How to Start Your Financial Future

You've Got to have the Why Before the How

Edward Gardner

Outskirts Press, Inc.
Denver, Colorado

The opinions expressed in this manuscript are solely the opinions of the author and do not represent the opinions or thoughts of the publisher. The author represents and warrants that s/he either owns or has the legal right to publish all material in this book.

How to Start Your Financial Future - You've Got to have the Why Before the How
All Rights Reserved.
Copyright © 2008 Edward Gardner
V3.0

Cover Photo © 2008 JupiterImages Corporation. All rights reserved - used with permission.

This book may not be reproduced, transmitted, or stored in whole or in part by any means, including graphic, electronic, or mechanical without the express written consent of the publisher except in the case of brief quotations embodied in critical articles and reviews.

Outskirts Press, Inc.
http://www.outskirtspress.com

ISBN: 978-1-4327-2039-1

Outskirts Press and the "OP" logo are trademarks belonging to Outskirts Press, Inc.

PRINTED IN THE UNITED STATES OF AMERICA

Table of Contents

Foreword		i
Chapter 1	Life Planning	1
Chapter 2	The B Word	15
Chapter 3	Family Photos	25
Chapter 4	Financial Planning Process	29
Chapter 5	Debt	35
Chapter 6	Child's Play	49
Chapter 7	Saving for College	57
Chapter 8	Scared to be in the market	69
Chapter 9	Procrastination	71
Chapter 10	Going for the Gold	75
Chapter 11	Stay the Course	79
Chapter 12	Cost of Inflation	83
Chapter 13	Emergency Fund vs. Savings	89
Chapter 14	Will you be able to retire	93
Chapter 15	So you're not married	95
Chapter 16	Secret Agents	99

Chapter 17	Managed Money	105
Chapter 18	Investing	111
Chapter 19	Risk	117
Chapter 20	Retirement	123
Chapter 21	Taxes	131
Chapter 22	Legal Documents	139
Chapter 23	Insurance	143
Chapter 24	It's up to you now	149
Tidbits		151

Foreword

"The greatest discovery of my generation is that human beings can alter their lives by simply altering their states of mind" Psychologist William James

Another book on money. Whoopee! Is this a book I should read? Will this book do anything to make me think or do things differently? It depends on what your attitude is. You can be given a diet to help you reduce your weight, but will only work if you are in the right frame of mind. Like at the Alamo, you have heard the famous line when Colonel Travis drew a line in the sand with his sabre and said that any man who crossed the line could avoid the final battle. Of course 'not a soldier crossed the line'. You can be like most who avoid the final battle or you could be the chosen few who want to make a difference in their life. They are fed up with where they are in life, they are tired of living paycheck to paycheck and they are worried about how much money they will have for retirement. In August, 2005 there was a net zero savings in America. This is a shame. We are the richest country in the world, yet we are the worst savers. We take so much for granted. In the words of H. Jackson Brown, Jr. "You must take action now that will move you toward your goals. Develop a sense of urgency in your life."

Think for a moment, most of us will work for 40-45 years to the age 65 to then fund another 20-30 years in retirement. Do you spend before you save? Do you think about your financial future? As I have told many clients, many of us have been taught to tithe (give 10%) to our place of worship. Have you been tithing to your future? Do you plan on having someone take care of you in your future? Do you plan on inheriting money? The one person you can count on is yourself. You can't count on Social Security, big business, or the government to take care of you! Do you want to live with your children when you retire? Most people change jobs 8 – 10 times in their lifetime. I am sure you know many people who are above average and they change jobs many more times than that. I had one client once between him and his wife they had almost 20 jobs in one year. It would be hard just waking up in the morning and remembering where you work. In the old days many of our parents told us to find a good company because they would take care of us in our retirement. Those days are gone. With so many job changes in the majority of American careers, less are qualifying for retirement benefits. Many companies are getting rid of their retirement accounts, and some companies are having trouble keeping with their financial commitments in their retirement programs.

So far in this book I have asked a lot of questions. Most people live day to day and don't face their future challenges. For the most part, they are too busy with their lifestyles. For some it is scary to think about the future, but for most of us it is the Big P word, "**Procrastination.**" For many of us, we are just plain scared to face reality. We can sit and watch reality shows, but the one reality show we need to view is our own future. Yes, we should do something, and we should do it now. I know, you don't know where to get started. You weren't taught in school or maybe there is not a how to book yet. Yada yada yada. We know that we should do something. We will take care of it tomorrow, next week, next month, and next year. We go to a college, or trade school and they teach us a profession, but most of us are not taught what to do with our money. I am sure most of you work hard for your money. Shouldn't your money work hard for you? Do you have family that depends on you? Will someone be there for you in the future if you are in need? We need to realize that our life is a time line. If you look at most businesses, there is considerable planning in their future. A business is in the business of producing revenue. It has operating expenses. It's goal is to bring in more revenue than expenses so that it has a net profit. We need to realize like a business, we are in the business of taking in money. We have wages, and money we earn on investments. We also have operating expenses, rent, utilities, transportation, insurance, savings etc., and the list goes on. Like a business we don't want to operate in the red. We need to have more money come in than we spend. We need to set money aside for emergencies and for future.

In this book we will have you go through a process of thought for the short and long term. We will have you participate in exercises to help you begin planning for your financial future. Are you ready? Get out some paper, something to write with, and begin with an attitude that you will succeed! You may fall and have stumbling blocks along the way, but you will succeed over time. You may not hit all your goals when you want them, some might take longer than you anticipated and some might come sooner. But you will be given a path that you can pursue to change your financial future. So let's begin..................

"**Never tell people how to do things. Tell them what to do and they will surprise you with their ingenuity.**" **George S. Patton**

CHAPTER One
Life Planning

Money ...is a person's personal energy reduced to portable form....It can go where he could not go; speak languages he could not speak; lift burdens he could not touch with his fingers; and save lives with which he cannot deal directly. (Harry Emerson Fosdick)

Have you ever really sat down and thought what you want to do when you grow up? What are your personal and family goals on a yearly basis for the next five years? Then plan these goals in five year increments. In fact, plan them out to at least age 90. Recent studies have shown that a couple who is 65 years old one might have one partner with a 50% chance of living to 85 and a 25% chance of living to 92. Most families will spend more time planning a family outing or family vacation than they will their financial future. Think of our life as a time line. At different intervals of our life we have life events. Most of us go backwards by picking the event and then worrying about financing the event. Many of us say, let's go the easy way, let's use a credit card. Better yet, let's take money in form of a loan or withdraw money early from a retirement account and not only pay taxes, but penalties. Wrong, wrong, wrong. Let's face it, the word retirement means those funds are put aside for your retirement. During this period that you probably will not be working, most of us will have to rely on what we have set aside for what we call the "golden years". Not only will we take funds needed for that period of our lives, but we will loose the opportunity for those funds to grow over a period of time. Imagine you use the following exercise. Take some time (ever get bored at home and wish you had something to do) and make a generic life plan of things you want in the future. Yes, situations change in our life. But like a tailor, you have to take in and take out. You have to have a base to work from. You need to have an outline of what you want to do and where you want to go in the future. Let's say today you decided that you are going to take your family to Disneyland. Don't you need to set a time when you are going to go? You also will set a roadmap if you are driving, or set a time when you are going to leave, decide where you are going to stay along the way, look at what roads you are going to take, and plan how long it is going to take for you to get there. Then while you are there what activities you are going to do, for how long and how you will come back from your destination? On any trip you take, there always are outside influences that make changes to what we had planned. Park closing, weather, construction, sold out tickets, and the list goes on. So we usually are flexible and go with the flow.

For the trip you take you also have planning on saving funds for the cost of the trip. You have a time frame to save and set specific goals along the way. Wow! we want to enjoy life and when something is that important to you, you make the time to plan it and also make financial sacrifices to make sure there is money to pay for it. We have a bigger trip we need to plan for, that is our life plan. We start at point A where we are today and we need to plan all the way to the end. There is no perfect plan and every plan will be changed. General George S. Patton once said: "An imperfect plan implemented immediately and violently will always succeed better than a perfect plan." We must plan for our financial future. We must realize that there will be no perfect plan as we have a lot of outside influences that affect what we do. We have war, inflation, natural disasters, terrorism, job changes, family status, deaths, births, and the list goes on. Yet like planting a garden, when you plant seeds over time they grow into crops. We just need time for the seeds to grow. We all need to get on a pay as you go plan. Small amounts of money set aside over long periods of time will help you reach your financial goals. Take a birth of a child today. Let's say you start saving for college. I know that's 18 years from now. What if little Johnnie or Susie doesn't go to college or gets a scholarship? The worst thing that you did is have more money for your other goals. Isn't that better than asking where in the _____ I am going to come up with $ X to pay for college? Some interesting information, someone that gets a high school diploma will make about 40% more than someone who didn't graduate high school. Someone who gets a college degree will make over 80% more than someone who gets a high school diploma. This amounts to over $500,000 more over a lifetime.

So how do you begin a plan? You start by sitting down, thinking about your future and most importantly, putting it down on paper. See, when we just think about things, life gets in the way and we forget or put what is important to us on the back burner. Remember something you needed to do, you thought about it, forgot it, and later remembered it? Majority of the battle is putting it in writing. Have you ever written a note or a paper for school? You began with an outline or a draft and then made changes. You have to do the same thing with your financial goals. Goals change, you add new ones, and you discard old ones. So take a few moments before you go any further in this book and write down important things you want in the different phases of your life. I left a section at the end of this chapter to help you create what events are important to you. Before you can go any further in planning for your financial future you need to complete this exercise. Now don't cheat and read ahead. Take time now to write these items down. In fact, put it down for a day, sleep on them, and come back to see if there is anything you can add. You might want to get out a pad of paper or a notebook and start working on some of the exercises I will have you complete throughout the course of this book. If you are married or have a significant other, each one of you should do this exercise separately. Then talk about it together and combine how you see your future. In my opinion, there is nothing more important in planning your financial future than completing this exercise.

While you are working on this exercise I want you to role play. I want you to imagine that you are a producer. You are making a movie. Wouldn't that be fun? Think about it, you get to be creative. You will meet a multitude of people along the way. One thing, as a producer you get to be in control. For some of us, that might be the first time in your life. In making a movie, you get to review scripts. You get to see the movie evolve from the first scene to all the scenes along the way until the final scene. You get to give your input in making changes to the scenes. In creating a movie, they constantly make changes, flexibility is the key. So, let's think of a title of a movie we can make for you. Hm....... I have an idea, why don't we title the movie …. **"The rest of your life."** In this movie you will be the star, at your current age, and where you are currently in life. You will have to write a script showing where you are going in the near future, and all the way to the final act, when you die. Like any script there has to be a starting point and a final scene. You always start with a rough draft and then you go back and edit it. Your editing will be the rest of your life. If you are married or have a significant other, you both need to begin a draft separately. Then you will talk about it together.

If you are married or you have a significant other, both of your input is so critical and you need to each voice your independent opinion. After all, it is your life. But for this exercise to truly work, you need to do the exercise when you are most creative. Are you a morning, afternoon, or evening person? When do you have the most energy? That is when you need to work on this exercise. You want to do it when you are sharp, energetic, creative and not when you can barely keep your eyes open. You need to make a commitment to do this exercise within 48 hours. As I said earlier most of us will spend more time planning a family event (July 4th, Thanksgiving, Christmas, etc.) than our financial future.

In this exercise, I want you to write it down, not just think about it. I want you to write it down yearly for the next five years. What do you see yourself doing, things you will be doing for your children, parents, or others you give financial support to. After five years I want you to go in five year increments all the way to age 90. As I said earlier, there are several studies showing that you have 25% chance of a married couple having one partner living to age 92. In this exercise write down when you want to retire. In retirement, write down what you will be doing, what type of lifestyle you will be living. So are you ready, quiet on the set! Ready, Action, Begin!……..

Note: In your life plan take a few moments to write down future events in each of the following categories. This is a quick list of important life events. It is important to write down in areas that apply to you what your wants and desires are for your future.

"I am a firm believer in goal setting. Step by Step. I can't see any other way of accomplishing anything." – Michael Jordan

How to Start Your Financial Future - You've Got to have the Why Before the How

_____ Life Plan

Marriage
Divorce 6/1

Birth of a child or time frame in having children

Elementary School Events

Extra Curricular Events

Hobbies:

Middle School Events

High School Events

College *4yr.*

Graduate School

Post Graduate

Career Choice/ Career Changes
Personal trainer/Pilates Gyrotonic Instructor manager

Edward Gardner

First Job
Line Studio Manager $65K

Is my job what I want, where should I go from here
Develop into administrator

First Home *Trying to purchase*

Vacations *TRAINING*

Second Home

Retirement

Grandchildren

Your extra curricular activities

Leaving a legacy for your spouse, significant other, family, or charity *yes / Kids college*

Parents

Add your other future goals

Now ask yourself a few questions:
How much are you currently saving each month ___0___
How much are you going now to save each month $1 80
How much would you like to see your net worth in
5 years:
10 years:
15 years:
Keep going until you reach age 65.........
By the way, net worth is the difference between what your assets are less your liabilities. This is also known as what your wealth is.

Now that I had you write down a list of life events, go to the exercise of how you see your life yearly for next five years and then five year increments. Get out some paper or a note pad to work on this exercise. You can do it, I am so proud of you. You are beginning a step toward improving your financial future.

Year 1 (put year, i.e. 2008)
Year 2 (year)
Year 3 (year)
Year 4 (year)
Year 5 (year)
Year 10, etc

Don't forget to write down the year that you want to retire. If along the way in the 5 year intervals you have a major life event, list the event and the year. For example, College – Johnny – 2012.

The exercise I have just had you do is to help you get your "**Why**" in life. That is, your sense of purpose and a map of what you would like to have and accomplish for yourself and your family. Some people will call these their family goals. One thing, goals are not only absolutely necessary to motivate us. They are essential to really keep us alive. (Robert H Schuller) To help us accomplish our life goals, we have to focus on the future. Insanity is doing the same thing over and over again and expecting different results (Albert Einstein). Once you have listed these life events I would like you to put how many years away before these events will occur. Remember when you were in school and you had a test. Let's say Friday morning at 10 am. When did you study for it? Most would say the night before or a few days before. If you didn't have a timeframe to study for the exam, would most of us really have studied? If we don't put down what we want to happen with life events in our life and time frame for them to happen, we loose focus in making sure that these events will become a reality by saving toward their costs. Of course, we can get out the old credit card and put ourselves further in debt. Recently, one of my clients invited me to their child's wedding. About 10 years ago I had them do this exercise. They had estimated at that time having to pay $ 20,000 for their daughter's wedding in about eight years. Reality is that the wedding occurred 10 years later and cost almost $ 28,000. By Planning Ahead With Ed and using this exercise, they were financial ready for this life event. They actually came out of pocket less than $ 1,000 from a previous estimate 10 years earlier. They were fortunate in that the investments they chose performed better than our conservative estimate of future earnings. In fact, they hadn't planned for it, but were able to give their daughter and their new son in law money for their honeymoon. By putting the funds away on a monthly basis, they were able to give the wedding that the family dreamed of. They even were able to send money for airfare and hotel rooms for family members who would not have come because of the cost. No one has a crystal ball and knows the exact time and amount future events will cost. But one thing for certain, it's better to be a little short or a little over in funds saved for any future family life event than not to have saved at all. So many people procrastinate and don't want to come to reality that a future event needs to have action taken today. I have learned from life that it's the little things that make a difference.

I know most of you have heard the quote "That's one small step for *a* man, one giant leap for mankind." These words were Astronaut Neil Armstrong's first words from the surface of the moon on July 20, 1969. You see in the statement I have the letter 'a' before man. The Web site www.slipups.com notes, "Mr. Armstrong's quote left out that ever important letter 'a'. His quote, 'One small step for man; one giant leap for mankind' should have been 'One small step for a man; one giant leap for mankind.' Without it he basically said 'One small step for mankind; one giant leap for mankind.'' For history buffs, there was an Australia-based computer programmer Peter Shann Ford. He did a computer analysis of Astronaut Neil Armstrong's statement. According to Ford, Armstrong spoke, "One small step for a man ... " with the "a" lasting a total of 35 milliseconds, 10 times too quickly to be heard."

In Armstrong's book First Man: The Life of Neil A. Armstrong, Armstrong stated "It doesn't sound like there was time for the word to be there. On the other hand, I didn't intentionally make an inane statement, and ...certainly the "a" was intended, because that's the only way the statement makes any sense."

Life passes us by so fast and we also don't intend not to plan for various life events. We get so caught up in our day to day lives, putting out fires at work, running errands, taking care of our children, family, etc. We know deep down about life events that will happen in the future, yet we stay focused on today and forget to also focus on tomorrow. The milliseconds we could spend on doing simple things to plan for our futures can change not only the quality of life we can have, but the stress and anxiety we will create down the road. Sure we need a little more time than a millisecond to plan, but put in the overall big picture, and it is like a millisecond in our time.

I remember a quote I once heard from a book by Denis Waitley, "There are two primary choices in life; to accept conditions as they exist, or accept the responsibility for changing them." I can't over emphasize that we need to see a map, a time line of what we want our future to be. What will happen in the future. By putting it down in print, bring the future to the present, we can take steps to prepare for them. Any event that you plan for before it happens in reality is retirement planning. I know you are thinking, what does saving for events before your retirement have to do with retirement planning? Think for a second. If you have an event and you haven't adequately saved for it, you may have to incur debt to fund the event or forgo the event (for example college education). If you incur debt, you will need future funds to retire the debt. These funds will not be able to be saved for your retirement or may cause debt to still be there when you retire.

So, why not go back just one more time and list life events you would like to see for your family. Then, list the number of approximate years to the time that that event will occur. Then draw on a sheet of paper a time line listing the event, year and number of years from now, and the estimated amount needed. You now have begun planning for your financial future. It may be a little scary, but as Donald Trump said in "Trump: Art of the Deal" "Money was never a big motivation for me, except as a way to keep score. The real excitement is playing the game." Your game is the game of life and winning by being able to have the various life events you want for your family.

Once you have a time frame and an estimated amount needed for a life event, you can calculate what is needed on a monthly or annual basis to help pay for that event. If you don't have access to a calculator to compute this, you can always go to our website www.planningaheadwithed.com. Go to calculators and you can put in the estimated future amount, estimated earnings and it will tell you how much you will need to save on a monthly basis to fund the event. A common question I get is: What if I don't have enough to put away each month to pay for the event? My answer is quite simple; when you were a small child to learn to walk you crawled first and then started taking baby steps at first. A habit, a crawl, a first step is to start funding your future life event by putting something away each month. As your income grows, you retire debt; you can increase the amount that you put away.

"You may be disappointed if you fail, but you are doomed if you don't try" (Beverly Sills)

CHAPTER TWO
The B Word

"Indecision leads to procrastination, procrastination leads to failure" (Napolean Hill)

Now that you have set some basic life events that you want in life, you realize that they will all have one thing in common – they all cost money. So where are you going to come up with the money? It all starts out with the B word; "**budgeting**" along with savings. I know for many the B word feels like a four letter dirty word. But let's have a paradigm shift in your thinking. I am sure you may have or know someone that has worked for a big company. The companies have different departments and each department has a budget on what they can spend. If one department spends too much, it will hurt the cash flow of the company.

If enough of overspending occurs, the company could have financial difficulties or even go bankrupt. So, consider yourself to be like a big company. You are in the business of bringing in revenue. You have budgets for different departments. Your goal is to bring in more money each month than what you spend. If you really analyze it, one of your departments is your emergency department. Another is savings for the future, retirement, hobbies, rent (mortgage), utilities, and so on. When you are a couple, different things are important to each person. For example, one partner may want to spend money on shopping each month. Another may want to spend money on hobbies (for example golf). The reality is that each area you spend on is important to you. You both work hard for your money. You deserve to spend money on things that make life enjoyable. But everything we do has to be done with moderation. You need to set a budget on what is a reasonable amount to spend each month. Many people get upset and to make themselves feel better, they go out shopping and buy things. It is like overeating when we are upset. It is a quick fix, a quick high, but in the end we put ourselves further in the hole. If we were watching our weight, we did the wrong thing by gorging ourselves. If we are in debt, we added to our problem. So congratulation, you are a mini big business. You have departments and you need to stay within the budgets for each department. You are not nagging at a partner on how they are spending. If you both agree to a limit on what you are spending in a particular area, then you now are facing reality. So where to begin, and how do you come up with what you should spend. When I have advised clients on how to review their spending, I had them complete the following exercise. First, I had you put in the first column heading the word "Budget". Some people prefer to use the word lifestyle instead of budget. Write it down in pencil (yes, pencil) what you think is a reasonable amount. Now add it up. For most of us we will be amazed at how much we spend each month. Before you go any further, calculate how much you deposit each month from your paychecks and any other sources of income into your checking account. A lot of us will find out that we are spending more than what we are bringing in. Do you see a problem here? Now, go back and take a second shot at what you think is reasonable to spend in the different areas each month so that you will not spend more than what you bring in.

Have you ever seen someone on a diet that lost weight, looked great, and then gained it all back? This can happen with this exercise. We are creatures of habit. Once we find an area that we have overspent in, we need to work on that area. We need to monitor our spending and make sure that we don't fall back into our old habits. A few minutes each month monitoring our spending will help keep us on track. I have a stone that I keep in my office to constantly remind me "Never Never Quit". We need to make it a lifetime goal to watch how we are spending.

You have now come up with what you should work toward spending each month. Now read the first two lines on the following Budget Worksheet. Read them out loud, Savings and Retirement. For most of us when we plan a budget we put these last. Take a pencil and roll it from the top of the page to the bottom. You will see that the pencil rolls off the page. It is out of sight, out of mind. When we don't put savings first and retirement first, we tend to put them where they fall off the page. In other words, we don't save and we don't put money aside for savings and retirement. My rules of thumb, if you are starting in your 20's, save at least 10% of what you make. If you are starting in your 30's, save at least 15% of what you make. If you are starting in your 40's, save at least 20% of what you make. Will this be enough? It depends on your lifestyle, your compounded earnings over time and in your retirement and the rate of withdrawals you make during retirement.

As part of your exercise, I would like you to go back 6 to 12 months and track where you have actually spent your money in different categories. Add them up for each month and put them on the worksheet. When we overspend, we are usually consistent and do it in a particular area. If you say that you will spend $150 on a hobby (or clothes shopping) each month and you see that you are spending $400, you are hurting the family. That's $250 a month, $3,000 a year. For most families, that is a lot of money. Benjamin Franklin once said "Beware of little expenses. A small leak will sink a great ship." Now let's have a paradigm shift in our thinking. No longer will you point the finger at your spouse and say see, I told you so. You now must tie savings to a life event in the future. Let's assume that you just gave birth to a child. You went to a favorite university (Ok, let's say University of Texas – I wonder what author went there?). You would like to see your child go there also. What if you put that $250 a month away for college? Do you know at 8% interest you would have around $80,000 when your child is 18? Could this make a big difference in whether your child attends college or not? See, when you first admit that you are overspending in a particular area that is your initial step. The most important thing is to have a reason, a goal to why you need to take the money you are currently spending and apply the funds elsewhere. Ok, so what if you make a smaller return or even a larger return, you now have a pile of money to help you for a major life event. Is looking into the eyes of your child and saying sorry we couldn't save money for you for college because shopping or a hobby was more important? When we have goals in life, financial goals, we see what is more important to us. Benjamin Franklin once said "a penny saved is a penny earned."

I remember one client who was a single mother and who was recently divorced. She had a beautiful 10 month old daughter. She wanted to save for college for her child. She had a decent job, but money was tight. In having her do this exercise, we saw that eating out was a lot more than what she wanted to budget each week. After talking with her, I found out that she stopped before and after work to a Coffee House to get a cup of coffee. She figured that she was spending about $7 a day. That's about $35 a week, and with simple math over $140 a month on coffee. Yet, she couldn't find $100 a month to put away for college. In talking with her she said she did it because everyone else in the office did it. So I came up with a solution. On payday, which was the 1st and 15th, she would go treat herself and get a cup of her favorite coffee. She would rinse the cup out and put regular coffee in it for the trip to work and back home. She now had the social prestige of that famous cup of coffee and she now saves $125 for college for her daughter. Going to college gave her a better opportunity and she wanted to do the same for her child. Just by prioritizing what is really important to her in life, analyzing where she was spending her money, now will make such a tremendous difference in her and her daughter's life.

A lot of us go out and buy things to impress people we know. Do you think they care about your financial situation? Do they care about you and your family? I remember one presentation I gave at the University of Houston Downtown campus for Black History month. I had an auditorium full of people who were older students. Many of them were in late 20's to early 30's. They had gone back to school to get their education they wanted for their future. For one reason or another, they couldn't attend college when they graduated High School. Most of the time they couldn't afford to go to college. In most cases, their families did not plan ahead for their college education. I had asked the group to imagine over a 15 year period how many cars they would own? The majority of those in the auditorium came up with about 5 cars, one every three years. They all listed off cars they could pay monthly for $800 a month and $500 a month. Many agreed that they would get the more expensive car as a status symbol to show off to other people. An interesting question I asked was do you remember the people you were trying to impress 15 years ago? 10 years ago? 5 years ago? Most people in the room agreed they couldn't remember. More important, I asked them if it really mattered now what their opinion was from these people. Everyone said no.

I then had them imagine if they had invested the $300 difference over a 15 year period. The room came up with a 7% return they thought would be a good average return. At the end of 15 years, they would have over $90,000 if $3,600 was saved once a year at the end of the year, or over $100,000 if saved monthly. Wow, what a difference an extra $90,000 could make to helping them meet their families' life plan. Could it help you save for college for a child, pay for a wedding for a child, or just have more money for your retirement or one of your life events?

Learn an important lesson here. You don't have to impress others. If they are true friends it doesn't matter what car you drive, and what toys you own. They want to be your friend and share with you their family and your family life events. Do you think Sam Walton cared about what people thought about him driving an old pickup?

So before you read any further in this book, take time to complete the exercise. If you are married, make sure you both agree on what is reasonable to spend each month in each category. Feel free to make your spending categories more detailed than what I show. In breaking down the expenses into categories, I would recommend that both of you work on this exercise individually. In a lot of households usually one spouse pays most of the bills. It is a good idea to have the other spouse help with the detail so they can see all the different places that you have to write checks and all the expenses you incur each month. Work on this exercise with an open mind. Many times couples turn off to what the other is saying about money. This is your life, your life plan, your chance to make a difference in your financial future. Be open, be companionate, and be a true partner to each other. I remember this last year when I spoke at the Power Tools meeting in Houston to a group of nonprofit organizations in Houston. A women came up to me after my speech. She said she was hesitant to come to my talk because having someone talk about money was something that was not of interest to her. She said that a friend had her come because she had heard my radio show in Houston. She listened with an open mind. She finally heard things that her husband was trying to say to her for years. She gave me a big hug and thanked me as she said I saved her marriage. She and her husband, like many couples, always fought over money. From my readings and talking with clergy, money problems are the number one issue that breaks up couples. She finally realized that her husband wasn't nagging her about her spending. She in fact was hurting herself, her two daughters, and her husband by overspending in a few areas. The reality here is that I didn't save her marriage. I was only a messenger sharing a message that most couples don't want to hear. She saved her marriage by listening and hearing what I had to say. She will save her marriage by taking action and making positive changes in her spending habits.

Will you listen and take action? Might be a good chapter to reread and follow through this exercise. In fact, this might be a good chapter to have your spouse or significant other read. I hope other couples will hear my message and their marriages will flourish. Though I used a story about a woman overspending, men need to look at themselves in the mirror and see where they can also make a difference.

BUDGET WORKSHEET

	BUDGET					
Savings – Retirement						
Security						
Automobile –						
Oil & Gas						
Repairs						
Books / Magazines						
Charitable Contributions	$150					
Clothing						
Dental						
Entertainment						
Food & Beverage						
Gifts						
Hobbies						
Household Maintenance & Repair						
Installment & Credit Card Payments						
Insurance Premiums -						
Auto	$168.00					

Health	$192/PAYCHECK DEDUCTION					
Life						
Loan Payments	0					
Medical	$105					
Miscellaneous						
Mortgage or Rent						
Personal Care						
Public Transportation						
Tuition						
Utilities & Fuel						
Electricity						
Gas or Oil						
Telephone						
Water						
Vacation						

A final thought. When it comes to using a budget (lifestyle) we all can be broken down into 4 basic groups First, are those individuals who are Impulsive. You tend to spend for today and for tomorrow well, tomorrow is another day and it will just take care of itself. A budget is the least of your concern. Then there are those who are deniers who refuse to admit that they are in financial trouble. So out of sight is out of mind and they refuse to admit that they need a budget. Strugglers are the third group that find it hard to keep what we could say "their head above water". And finally, if you utilize what I have suggested, are those that are Planners who have set their mind to controlling their financial affairs. A planner will budget to improve their lifestyle. They will put their future of their family, their loved ones, their significant others first.

I'm so proud of you for working on the budget! Just remember, like any type of weight loss program, you need to monitor it and don't get back into bad habits. What you have created you need to review each month and in areas that you go overboard, you need to say " I am proud of what I have accomplished. I know that this area I need to make improvements and in the next month I am going to do the following with this area. I will improve my spending in this area by…………………(you know how you need to answer each area)." Be proactive, stop the bleeding in your spending before it gets out of hand again.

Lack of money is the root of all evil "George Bernard Shaw"

CHAPTER Three
Life Planning

Every day someone celebrates family birthdays, anniversaries, and life events. Someone is there to take pictures so your family will have a snap shot of family life events. Isn't it interesting how important it is for us to keep a record of these events? Scrap books are made, pictures are taken, videos, cards, letters, all types of items are kept from these events. Then we come to something we all have, our money. It is amazing how many people can't answer or even come close at guessing "How much do you have in savings, and retirement accounts?"

Most of America lives for today and either procrastinate or don't want to face what they should do about their future. Have you ever thought about taking a snapshot of where you are financially? NO, that doesn't mean take a picture of cash in your wallet. What I am saying here is to record a specific time, (monthly, quarterly, or annually) all your assets and liabilities and see what your net worth is. NO, you don't have to go to the local university and take accounting 101. You should take the time to list all financial assets and see if they are growing or declining in value. You should list what debt you have. Is the debt growing or are you retiring debt. Your children in school from time to time get a report card to see what progress they are making. Shouldn't we as adults do the same thing? How can we monitor where we are if we don't take the time to do this. I know you live a busy life. You have a full day at work, household chores, and activities with the family. Let's not forget about the time in front of the television. There is always an excuse. But we are like a small business as I said earlier. Any business will have money for security, retirement, and operating reserve. Don't they constantly monitor to see where they are? See what I am saying. This is one of the biggest problems for the average American family. You do not take the time to monitor where you are. So as a guide, I have set up categories on the following page. Make a copy of this page or better yet, build it on a spreadsheet in a program like Microsoft Access, or Microsoft Excel.

	Account Number	Date – as of	Date	Date	Date
Cash at Bank					
CD's					
Investment Account					

Cash Value Life
Insurance

Notes Receivable

Retirement
Account

Real Estate

Outside
Investments

Vehicles

Credit Cards

Notes Payable

You will never know how to get to where you want to go without first understanding- and being totally honest about – where it is you are starting from (Brian Kay)

CHAPTER Four
Financial Planning Process

Happiness is not in the mere possession of money; it lies in the joy of achievement, in the thrill of creative effort. (Franklin D Roosevelt). We have an opportunity to improve our families' future just by taking a few steps. Financial Planning does take a little effort and work on your part. As Thomas Edison stated "Opportunity is missed by most because it is dressed in overalls and looks like work" The best thing about the future is that it only comes one day at a time (Abraham Lincoln). To accomplish great things, we must not only act, but also dream; not only plan, but also believe. (Anatole France). Most of us live day by day and don't plan for our financial future. Then one morning, we wake up and wonder where and how we will financially continue on. If you don't know where you are going, you can never get lost (Herb Cohen). We must invest the time to plan for our future. Change is the law of life. And those who look only to the past or present are certain to miss the future. (John F. Kennedy)

We have a choice to make it another do it yourself project. We can open up the paper, get magazines, and read about where to invest. One word of caution, what was a good investment last year just might not be a good investment this year. Some publications will provide you with old news. Some publications will write about certain areas of investments and at the same time miracle of miracles, have advertisers of companies that sell that particular product advertise that month. Some columns are written by individuals that have no formal training in investments other than the school of hard knocks. I know of one person that was a food critic and their paper opened up a position for a financial writer. Since he was good at adding up tips, I guess that made him qualified. Yes, you can do it yourself. But most of us have been taught a trade or profession, and not taught what to do with our money.

So what is the financial planning process and should we use someone to help us? I am prejudice, but I believe that you should use a financial planner. Most of us will go to a professional (doctor, lawyer, accountant, etc) to assist us in their area of training. We do not personally have the time and training to keep current and learn from all the various options we have.

The Certified Financial Planner Board of Standards, Inc states that the process has six steps:

1. Establishing and defining the client-planner relationship
2. Gathering client data, including goals
3. Analyzing and evaluating your financial status
4. Developing and presenting financial planning recom-

mendations and/or alternatives
5. Implementing the financial planning recommendations.
6. Monitoring the financial planning recommendations.

You might find it interesting that I did not begin with this chapter for this book. I tried to take a different approach in guiding you through the financial planning maze. I actually had you start with step 2 – Gathering client data, including goals. I had you start with your "Why" in life. Without establishing your "Why", the process of working on your financial future will not allow you to follow through. I had you develop a life plan of what you wanted and needed for you and your family. I then had you see where you were spending your money and where you needed to trim some of the fat. Step 3 – Analyzing and evaluating your financial status – this is where I had you take a family photo of where you were with your assets and liabilities. Now let's discuss step 1 – Establishing and defining the client-planner relationship. To have this relationship you need to seek out someone to be your coach, your mentor. This choice is as important as making any investment decision you make. You want to find a person that you trust, you feel is knowledgeable, and has your interests as their number 1 concern in your relationship.

One of the best starting points is to ask other people you know on who they have used. Check the planner out with their associations to see if there is anything negative about their reputation. For some, you might start listening to financial programs on Talk Radio. For example, with my show (Planning Ahead with Ed, AM 650, KIKK- Houston), our focus is to help educate the typical investor. To provide them with information about different areas that affects them so that they can make intelligent decisions. You also want to check out the planner's credentials. There are several, but a few I think that are important to help you know that they have had advanced training are: CFP®, PFS, CPA, CHfc, CLU, and CSA.

What do these designations mean? First of all, they have gone through extensive training in their area. They require the individual to have experience in the area under the supervision of others already holding that designation. They have ethical standards that they must adhere to and also have ongoing continuing education so they keep current in their area the designations cover. So for those who have seen the designations and don't know what they mean, here is a short summary.

CFP® - Certified Financial Planner – 888-237-6275
    www.cfp.net
PFS - Personal Financial Specialist – 888-777-7077
    pfp.aicpa.org
CPA - Certified Public Accountant – 615-880-4200
    www.nasba.org/nasbaweb.nsf/mem
CLU - Charter Life Underwriter - 888-263-7265
    www,theamericancollege.edu
Chfc - Charter Financial Consultant - 888-263-7265
    www.theamericancollege.edu
CSA - Certified Senior Advisor – 800-653-1785
    www.society-csa.com

There are a lot of quality people that do not have these designations. However, I feel that if someone is serious about their profession, they obtain further education in their field. When you meet with a planner feel free to ask them questions about their background and for references. How many years have they been in practice? What type of educational background do they have and current education? What professional organizations are they affiliated with?

When you have selected a financial planner to help you, understand that it is an ongoing process. You might have them only assist you with one part of your financial plan. Then again, you might want to have them assist you with your whole financial plan. In this case, you will need to have ongoing communication with the planner.

It is important that the planner that assists you is independent. As an analogy, I am sure you have been to a cafeteria at one time in your life. At the cafeteria, you have a menu with different categories. Each category has several selections. The menu does not have everything, but it has a good variety. That is what you want with someone that is assisting you with your financial affairs. If they are helping you pick financial products, then you want to make sure that they are not representing only one company. It is like taking a square peg and trying to put it in a round hole. You want them to be able to take you, the consumer, to the market place. When you go shopping, the average person goes to several stores before they purchase the item. You want the planner to do the same for you. Some companies are more competitive in cost or yields in some areas. You need a planner that is not only knowledgeable and has your best interest at heart, but will shop to find you the best products.

There are some myths about financial planners that I feel need to be addressed. Financial Planners are not the same as stockbrokers. They also are not the same as insurance agents. True, some can be both; however the financial planner's main objective is to help you take your goals and help you achieve your goals and financial objectives. The function of most stockbrokers and insurance agents is to sell financial products. With a planner, some are fee based, commission based, and others charge for setting up a plan. When they set up a plan they may not sell you any securities, or insurance products. Financial Planners work with all size clients. Some will only work with the affluent, however, most work with the average American family.

Steps 4, 5, and 6 of the financial planning process are completed through the guidance of the financial planner and the team of other professionals that are assisting you plan for your financial future. It is important that you review your plan periodically to make sure that you have made changes when your financial circumstances or life events have changed (births, deaths, marriages, divorces, job loss or retirement)

CHAPTER Five
Debt

Creditors have better memories than debtors.
~Benjamin Franklin

There is good and bad debt to have. Some debts are fun when you are acquiring them, but none are fun when you set about retiring them "Ogden Nash". We need to learn the difference between **needs** and **wants**. We are the richest country in the world. We as Americans take so much for granted. Those that are immigrants coming to our country many times appreciate the opportunities we have more than those born in the US. I am sure that you have seen that baby with those beautiful big eyes when they are born. Many of us still have those big eyes as we turn into adults. Yes we need to have food and shelter to survive.

But do we need to have that fancy car, boats, planes, expensive clothes, etc. Quite often we get them to keep up with others in our circle of friends and acquaintances. Or, we purchase just to impress others. Maybe, it just makes you feel good. I have seen people who have financial troubles, get laid off from a job, go out and buy something to make them feel good. I have seen teenagers and adults that when they spend the day at a shopping mall to occupy their time and be with friends have to buy something. Have you ever heard of window shopping? I remember a friend once told me that he went with his wife to shopping malls after 9 pm and let her buy anything she wanted. Of course, the stores were closed.

We as consumers need to stop the "high" we get with shopping, and stop shopping only for our wants. We need to realize that debts and lies are generally mixed together (Francois Rabelais). We are lying to ourselves that we will pay for the item. Remember two years ago this past Saturday when you were at the shopping mall, you went with your friend and had that wonderful lunch? Do you remember where you went? Do you remember what you ate? For many Americans, they are still paying for that lunch. They paid a tip to the waiter or waitress. But they didn't factor in the interest they are still paying on the balance for that lunch. Buying on credit is much like being drunk. The buzz happens immediately, and it gives you a lift. The hangover comes the day after (Dr. Joyce Brothers). Debt is the slavery of the free (Publilius Syrus). One of our great leaders of our country Thomas Jefferson once said "Never spend your money before you have it". When we do this, we loose the opportunity of accumulating wealth to help us with our life plan. When we have too much debt, we loose the ability to have ample funds available for our needs in our life, shelter, food, transportation, education, health costs, and retirement.

A study made by Cardweb showed that the average American household has 13 payment cards. These payments are for department stores, credit cards, and debt cards. The U.S. Dept of Health & Human Services estimate that 96% of all Americans will retire financially dependent on the government, family, or charity. There is a problem here. If we don't change our ways, we will live a life as Ralph Waldo Emerson once said "A man in debt is so far a slave". The Federal Reserve has found that over 40% of US families spend more than they earn. There has been studies that found when we use a credit card we **spend 112% more** on a credit card purchase than if we paid by check or cash.

Holiday time is a prime example. I have told clients and on radio to be part of my Holiday Club. Starting in January every year set $ 20 a week aside for holiday gifts. By the holiday season, you will have around $ 1,000. The average American incurs around $ 713 in debt for holiday gifts. First things first, if you had a wound on your arm and it was bleeding, what would you do? Of course, you would do whatever you could to stop the bleeding. That is what we need to do with our debt. We need to stop the bleeding. Take those credit cards and lock them up. Why put more wood on the fire if you are trying to put the fire out. For holiday gifts, if you are in debt, I will give you a hint. Your family and friends probably are in debt also. Approach them before the holidays and talk and be candid. Tell them that you have a lot of debt and that you are trying to retire the debt. You would like them to agree that for the next year for birthdays, holidays, etc. that you will either not exchange gifts at all or set a dollar limit. Children are children and they don't understand. Sure you will still celebrate holidays and birthdays for children with gifts. But everything needs to be done in moderation. I have seen when a child is born. Parents, grandparents, brothers, sisters, and friends go crazy on buying toys and clothes. A question to ask you, does a child under three, four, or even five really remember all the items that you have given them? If you are a parent, don't go crazy on buying all these items for the child. That is only putting you further in debt.

    I remember once I was in Dallas, Texas on business for a client. This client had a large beautiful home and asked that I stay at their home. In working with him, he was trying to get out of debt. Since I was there for a few days working on a project for him, I appreciated that he wanted to save the cost of the hotel room. But something I saw hit home about his overspending like many parents. When we left the first morning, he had to take his 7 year old son to school. That day at school was show and tell. Each child would bring something and tell the other children about it. In a game room, there was two play pin full of toys. The child stood in the room staring at the toys for a few minutes and began to cry. His dad went over and the child told him he couldn't decide what toy to bring because he had too many toys to pick from. His dad picked one and we went on our way for the day. Something I learned here and hope you do too, is that we are a country of abundance. We want to have it all. We want to let our children have things that maybe our parents couldn't provide for us when we were small. We want to please our children, spouse, parents, and family. But are we doing the right thing. Are we teaching them young about just getting something because we want it or need it? I would estimate that the two play pins had several thousand dollars of toys the parents had bought for the child. The reality is that the child only played with most of the toys a few times. Then they sat there and collected dust. I wonder if the funds had been set aside, what they could have done with one of his life plan events.

I experience a single mother one time that a friend had dated. She had a 7 year old daughter, and barely got by financially each month. Every month my friend wanted to buy a toy for his girlfriend daughter. After he did it once, she asked him not to do it except for her birthday or holidays. He asked her why. She said that her daughter had about a dozen toys. She would take out half each week and her daughter would play with them. Then she would put them away and take out the other toys the next week. Her child was happy, felt loved, and now has turned into a wonderful young woman. Items for you pet is another area that I have seen consumers go crazy. When I have been at various homes, many had a pet for their children. There usually was a box full of toys and a few toys scattered around the house. Then once, I saw a client recently divorced with a child that had a cat. She had two toys for her pet. The animal wagged their tail constantly, tail raised high in the air and was happy playing with the same toy. I will end with one quote from Eric Hoffer; "You can never get enough of what you don't need to make you happy".

Be aware of debt in our country is important also. On a website www.treasurydirec.gov they show the outstanding public debt as follows on September 24, 2007 –

Current	Debt Held by the Public	Intragovernmental Holdings	Total Public Debt Outstanding
09/24/2007	5,066,560,425,665.34	3,927,135,388,792.57	8,993,695,814,457.91

To show you the impact of our economy, just one decade earlier as of September 24, 1997 the total public debt outstanding was $ 5,384,224,726,974.01. An increase in one decade of our national debt of over 3.6 billion dollars. As of July 23, 2007, not quite the date of these figures, the population in the United States was 302,419,072. This means that there is about $ 29,739 of total public debt per person in the US. Alan Greenspan said "I must say, I never expected to see the day where I would be talking about anything other than reducing the debt; I'm running into the tyranny of zero, which this where you can't reduce (the debt) any more". It is important also in reviewing debt to look at how our local, state, and federal governments spend money. Don't be passive and only voice your opinion by complaining to your friends and family. Band together with others and voice your opinion and demand changes. It only takes one to get another to make a change.

Creditcards.com did a study and found that the average credit card account interest rate was 13.46% as of May 2007. The Federal Reserve stated that the average medium income of a U.S. household is currently $ 43,200 and their typical credit card balance is about 5% of their annual income. Cardweb.com, a service that tracks credit card trends, shows that average American household with at least one credit card was $8,940 in 2002. Averages mean that several are less, but several are substantially higher. There is good news; about 24% of American households have no credit cards at all. The Federal Reserve Bank of Philadelphia estimates that approximately 40% of the credit card users pay their balance in full each month as of a study for 2007. Myfico.com states that the average consumer has a total of 13 credit card obligations on record at a credit bureau. They state that about 9 are likely to be credit cards s and 4 are likely to be installment loans. Let's take $ 8,940 in credit card debt. If you paid only $ 134 a month, at 18% interest, you would only pay the interest each month. In reality, you would never pay off the debt. What if you paid $ 200 a month? You would take 6 years to pay off your balance and incur interest of $ 5,973. Want to figure out how long to pay off your current credit cards. Go to my website www.planningaheadwithed.com. Go to calculators, loans and credit cards, and then go to credit card debt. Fill in the information and see what a few extra dollars each month can do in retiring the debt. You might want to keep this site as a favorite. Every month we add new articles, and newsletters. There is a glossary of financial terms, and even some e-seminars. You can get quotes on your stocks. And, there is a picture of yours truly (no comments).

Some ways of getting out of debt-

1. Stop spending – you need to commit to change. Set a goal to pay off your debt within a certain time frame. Take a credit card with a smaller balance. Set a short term time frame to pay it off. Like a diet, when you see success, losing a few pounds, you feel better and know you are on the road to obtaining your goal. Paying off that balance will give you a sense of accomplishment and begin retiring your debt. Take the monthly payment that you were making on that credit card and now add it to a payment on another credit card. Take your credit cards and either put them away in a safe place or destroy them.
2. Make a list of what debt you have, the amount that you owe, what interest rate that you are being charged. Go to my website and see how long it will take to pay off each credit card debt.

3. Contact you various credit card companies and see if you can get the interest rate reduced. It is like asking someone out, they either say yes or no.
4. In a separate call, ask your credit card company if they have balance transfers at a better interest rate. This could be good and at same time be bad. You might be able to transfer debt from a credit card with a higher interest rate to that of lower interest rate. It is important that you make at least the same amount of monthly payment as you were before on the two credit cards to retire the debt early. You need to put away the old credit card. Yes, lock it up. If you have a safety deposit box, put it in the box. It will do you no good to start running up a new balance on that card. When you transfer debt it is important to ask the credit card company if they charge any transfer fees. Do they have the reduced interest for a period of time or until the debt is retired? If you have a balance on that card from other charges, how do they apply the monthly payment? Most credit card companies will credit the payment on the lower interest debt first. If the card you now have your debt on has higher or the same interest as the card you are retiring the debt, you are not coming out ahead. Read the fine line on these offers. Here is where consumers get in trouble by transferring debt.
5. Have a garage sale – turn what is junk in your home into dollars. Take the funds and payoff the loans with the highest credit card interest first. Maybe there are some items you can put in a resale store and get a little more for the items. You might also consider selling items you no longer need on websites like ebay.
6. Reduce your monthly expenses. We can do anything for a short period of time. If you have a lot of debt,

could you help yourself by not buying anything unless it is a **need** for a period of time? I am sure you can go through your closet and find outfits that you haven't worn in a while. You can also look to mix and match outfits that still will have you in style.
7. Debt consolidation – you might look at having a home equity loan, short-term bank loans or mortgage refinancing to help retire debt. Advantage is that you consolidate several loan payments into one loan payment. The finance charge would be reduced. Payments more often than not will be reduced. Here is where you can get ahead. If you make the same total payment you had in the past, you will retire the debt faster. Again, put these credit cards away. You don't want to add to your debt.
8. Track your spending every month. It is hard to change habits but easy to go back to your old ways.
9. Consider paying with cash instead of a credit card. This will help you spend less than if you had charged a purchase on a credit card.

There is actually good debt that we may have. Debt on items that have the opportunity to appreciate are good to have debt on. So is debt on items that have tax advantages to them. The most common form of good debt is your home. Wait a second, my parents told me to pay off my home? In fact, your grandparents may have told you the same thing. Let's take a walk back to the time of the great depression. The stock market crash occurred on October 29, 1929. At that time, most of the financing for homes was through banks. At that time, banks could call a loan at will. When banks ran out of money, they then looked to the mortgage loans. They asked our grandparents and their friends to payoff the balance on their homes. Many didn't have the funds available and lost their homes. With their experience they told our parents who told us to pay our homes off early. But times change, mortgages change, and now loans on homes don't have the provision to be called at will. The fear that was instilled in our parents has been passed on to us. The fear of having a mortgage may cause you to loose your home. The average mortgage is held about 5 years. If you think about it, most people never pay off their mortgage. Most of America will refinance a mortgage.

When someone talks about paying off a mortgage early, I like to ask them two questions. First, let's assume that you pay an extra $100 a month on your mortgage payment. Did that payment have any impact in the value of the house going up or down? Now let's assume that you have two banks. Bank A pays no interest and Bank B pays a little. Where would you put your money? Of course, in Bank B. By putting more money into the house, it in fact does not increase the value and does not increase the rate of return on your investment in your home. If someone put $10,000 down on their home and it goes up $10,000 in value, they have made a 100% return on their money. What if you instead put extra money into your home to try to pay it off early? Let's say you have now put $50,000 into your home. Yes you have more equity in your home when you sell because you had put another $40,000 into your home. But it is your return that is important. You only made a 20% return on your money ($10,000 increase in value/ the $50,000 you invested in your home.) You also put additional money into an investment that will rise or decline in value regardless of how much you have invested in it. What if the real estate market is declining and the value of your home goes down? You now have opportunity cost of the potential loss of additional return on the extra money you have put into your home. What if you got laid off at work and need additional funds to help meet living expenses until you find a new job or sell your home. It is hard to take the brick off the side of the house to pay your house note, feed your family, get a tank full of gas, etc. You also had no additional tax benefits by paying off your principal balance on your mortgage.

In my example, what if you took that extra $40,000 and invested it somewhere that gave you the opportunity of making a return. If the value of your home declined, you still would have these funds. True the funds could be invested and they have a positive yield or maybe they are invested and you loose some of your principal. But hear you have the opportunity of making money on these funds. You might say that by putting more money in the house, you reduce the principal balance and lower the interest you pay on your home. Making money and saving money on the interest are two different things. Since you are not increasing your return on your home by retiring your loan balance, you loose your opportunity to get a return on these funds.

About 2 years ago I had a client that came in with his spouse. He had exercised options on his company stock and had about $500,000 net of taxes. He wanted to payoff the balance of his mortgage of about $180,000. I went over the examples I gave you and we came up with another option. He set aside $180,000 in a blend of mutual funds with the understanding that if they went down in value to $160,000 he would sell the mutual funds and payoff his mortgage. Two years went by; he had a balance of about $165,000 on his mortgage. He of course, paid an extra $250 a month on his mortgage payment. He couldn't just let the normal monthly payment be paid.

The mutual funds that we invested in were worth about $240,000 at the end of the two years. He had made about $60,000 on the $180,000, a positive growth of about 33% and used money from his wages that were worth less to payoff his debt. You see, inflation causes the value of money we have to be worth less over time. His home went up in value about 4% a year in the area he lived. It went up regardless of the amount that he paid off on his principal balance. The extra $6,000 he paid over two years could have been invested to have a potential positive yield. What if the market had gone the other way, he still had a plan to get out and payoff his debt. Can you see the difference how debt on a mortgage on your home can be good debt? The same can hold true for investment property (rental property). You are using money of your renter to pay off your debt and help create potential equity in the property (assuming the value goes up).

Something else to consider is that Cash is King. You have cash available to take investment opportunities that come up that you would not be able to participate in if the funds were tied up in your mortgage. This could enable you to purchase more real estate, put more into your tax deductible retirement accounts, bridge the gap in emergencies, and etc., etc., etc.

Interest payments that you make on credit cards are not deductible. However, interest payments that you make on your personal residence are deductible if you itemize on the schedule A. Likewise, if you have rental property, you can take a tax deduction for the interest on the rental property. Rental property has some limitations on taking a loss on your return when you make over $100,000

Something interesting for you to know when a debt collector bothers you about nonpayment of a credit card debt that is quite old. Each state has a statute of limit where a debt becomes uncollectible. A debt collector may offer you discounts if you pay within a certain period of time. My recommendation is to have the debt collector provide in writing who was the original debt with, the original account number, amount of original debt, and history of payments. To find out the rules in your state go to www.fair-debt-collection.com/SOL-by-State.html.

Free from debt is free from care – Chinese proverb

CHAPTER Six
Child's Play

When the history of guilt is written, parents who refuse their children money will be right up there in the Top Ten – Erma Brombeck

You probably have heard stories of how a parent, aunt, uncle, friend had to walk miles to go to school. When they went to college they worked several jobs to pay for the expenses. I remember walking home from Junior High School about 1 ½ miles since I stayed after school to play football. I also worked several jobs to pay for college as my father had passed away when I was in High School. Like most parents, I wanted to make sure that my children would have a better lifestyle and more than what my parents were able to afford to give to me. Isn't that what we all want?

But, too much abundance for children can have a double edged sword. We can give and give and give to our children, yet they loose out on the experience and life lessons of working for what they want. They could loose at a young age that drive and determination that could be beneficial to them when they are adults. You have heard the stories of the trust fund babies that have it all. That is, until they spend it all. Now, what do they do? I hear story after story about clients who have wealth, send their kids to the best private schools, tell me about problems with friends of their children and maybe, just maybe, their own children. Money we have heard over and over can't buy happiness. Money doesn't show us how to earn it or how to take care of ourselves when we have no money. You have heard about millionaires that when they first started failed, then failed again, and failed again. They were one step away from success, they just didn't know how close or far away they were from success.

So, where do you start? What should you do or not do about money with your children. Understand, what you teach them will stay with them for a life time. Are you ready to really listen, are you sure. It may be different than what you might expect. One thing for sure, you will help put them on solid foundation that will set a stage for a better financial future.

The start – you buying all those toys, cute clothes and things that are so adorable. Do you remember all those things when you were an infant, 2, and 3 – even 6 years old? Probably not. Did they get worn once, twice, and put in the play pin or clothes cabinet. Why not consider that just maybe you are filling up a room full of items that cost hundreds, no thousands of dollars. Let's think for a minute, what if you talk to family and friends about them considering helping add to a college fund for your future president, athlete, and astronaut or .... Instead, you should consider not buying toys all the time for your children. Take a $1,000 put away when the child is one year old. At a projected 8% return, every 9 years the money will double. So $1,000 grows to $2,000 then to about $4,000 when the child goes to college. I am sure they will remember what that does a lot more than the toys and few extra cute outfits that get worn once and then put away. When a child can really appreciate that gifts were given to them, which do you think they will remember and appreciate more. The cute outfit they wore once, threw up on, you couldn't get the stain out, and it sat in a drawer. Or, the college fund created by their aunts, uncles, brothers, sisters, grandparents, friends, and others.

Now the child grows up, no longer an infant, and out of their mouth comes the word "allowance". Show me the money! I am cute, I can pout, and I will have my way! Of course, who is giving you an allowance? Do you have to work for a living? Do you have to earn the money that you bring home each month? Why not, are you ready to hear this......? Get rid of the word allowance. What should you use instead, gift, donation, no........ your child needs to learn that word you use....... WORK. Why not at a young age let them know that they have a job to do each day, each week and they will get paid for their work. Their job could be to pick up their toys, clean their room (don't get out the white gloves), take out the trash, help with the dishes, and mow the yard............ If they do their chores around the house, they will get paid X for their work. Who knows, they may want some extra money, then they may ask "Mom, Dad if I work more, can I get paid more. They might be creative and think of other ways they can earn money. This might not seem like much, but it begins a foundation of self worth, motivation, and leads to goal setting.

Now here is an interesting thought, your child may come to you and say I want this, I want that. It only costs $50, etc. Why not consider with a come back, "Ok, so this cost $50, how much of it are you going to pay for, from the work that you do?" I told the story earlier of my father having me pay some money for the baseball glove I wanted. Sure, he paid for most of it. But, by having me pay for some of it, I had the excitement and sense of accomplishment of doing something (working) for my new glove. Sure I could have said it is my glove without working for the glove. Yet, I took better care of the glove and it meant more to me because I shared in the cost. The same sense of pride will become part of your children's beliefs. I learned that being determined, saving for something I wanted, that in time, I could pay for it.

Now the years tic by and your child becomes a teenager. All their friends have this particular electronic device, name brand clothes; and they have to be like everyone else. Teaching them at a young age to work for and save for what they want will help them for their lifetime. Sure, a child's eyes will always be bigger than the pocket book. It is always easier to spend other people's money. Here you can start teaching them about budgeting. Teach them that when we work we are in the job of bring money home for the services we provide. That we need to have money available to pay for rent, insurance, groceries, clothing, medicines, and everything else we need to live. But we need to set aside money for emergencies, for savings for future, for retirement, and maybe give back to the community (to charity). Some parents who use this approach will not bring up what I am about to share until a child is a teenager. I personally feel that this lesson can be taught at a younger age. So what is the concept?

When a child earns money teach them that they have to

put the money in three places. First, teach them that part needs to go to charity. This could be to your place of worship, or some charity. Talk to them about how there are people who are not as fortunate as you are. How they need help. Let them learn at an early age the feeling of helping those less fortunate than you. Maybe consider having them bring a toy, clothes, or money to a charity drive. What better way than to learn as a youth.

The second area is to put part of the money to savings. Teach them that they have to save at least 10% to savings for future. You can go into the variety of reasons why it is important to save for their future. At that age, you might consider having them save a lot more than 10%. At that age, they will want to spend it all and then some. Take your child to the bank and open up a savings account with them. Teach them how to make a deposit and put money in an account at the bank. When the statements come in let them see by saving money, that it earns interest and helps their money grow over time.

The third area is money that they actually spend. Here you can teach them to budget how they spend their money and how to set priorities about what they spend their money on. If they want something, teach them that they may have to put money aside in savings until they have enough to pay for the item. Also, by setting the money in savings it grows and earns interest.

To make this really work, you have to be consistent, don't bend or waiver, and teach them that they have consequences for their actions.

When a child is young, I always like to recommend that you start teaching them about shopping. When they go to get gifts, let them know that you only have for example $20.00 this month to spend on toys. Show them the newspaper, flyers from stores and teach them to start to comparing the various toy store advertisements for prices on the toys. Discuss with them various ways of checking prices for toys. Go over not just getting in a car and drive to a store. Explain to them not only the value of time wasted, but cost of gas, etc. When they want something, go over is that within the budget and how they checked out the price.

Another exercise to do with a child is to have them create a business. For example, opening a lemonade stand. Go over the costs associated when you set up a business (materials, supplies, labor) and what profit they want to make. Let them help decide what they need, making signs, and selling the product. Though you won't get rich off this venture, you will create such a wealth in knowledge for your child.

Now comes High School, maybe consider having your child open up a checking account. Some areas will require you to wait to 18 before an account can be opened, yet other areas will allow you to have a joint account. Here you can teach them how to record the transactions and how to reconcile a bank account. I would talk with your officer to see if you can have an overdraft protection. Be sure to keep a close watch over the account. Should your child overdraft, show them how they will incur extra charges. Also, discuss with them how this can affect their credit. A good learning experience would be to have them go to the bank, meet with your bank officer, and make them apologize about the account over drafting. Hopefully you will get them to say that it will not happen again. That few dollars for an overdraft could change how they think about their checking account and how they treat it for their lifetime. It would be great if you could have a separate discussion with your officer and have them share with your child if it happens again, they will have to close their checking account.

As they are going through the High School years, start

How to Start Your Financial Future - You've Got to have the Why Before the How

discussing the costs associated with college. Have them sit down with you and have them along with you set up a budget for the costs of college. To tell someone how much something costs without them writing the checks loses in the translation how much something actually costs. By having them sit down with you, having them write down the amounts for each area, having them add up the costs for each month, will have a bigger impact.. Each semester costs change, so have them sit down with you and make changes to the budget. Let them see how much it costs each month, semester, and year. Let them see how much is set aside for college, if you will have enough, or if you will have to get loans. Teach them about inflation and how the same thing we buy today will cost more in the future. Teach them that they will have to set up budgets for the rest of their Lifetime.

College Cost Year 1	June	July	August	Sept	Oct	Nov	Dec	Jan	Feb	March	April	May
Tuition												
Books												
Deposits												
Dorm												
Insurance												
Health												
Auto												

Edward Gardner

Clothing										
Car										
Note										
Gas										
Charity										
Entertain-ment										
Food										
Gifts										
Hobbies										
Medical										
Rent (Dorm)										
Utilities										
Electric										
Gas										
Water										
Vacation										
Total										

CHAPTER Seven
Saving for College

Education costs money, but then so does ignorance
– Sir Claus Moser

Let's see, college is a long way off for my kids. Did you know that I paid for college myself? Have them get a job. Just a few of the many excuses I have heard over the years. A few facts about college that might be interesting to you:

There are about 4,084 institutions of higher learning that grant college degrees and it is projected that 2.7 million degrees will be granted in the 2005- 2006 academic year. There are 27% of the US adults over the age of 25 today that have at least a bachelor's degree. A study done in 2003 " The College Cost Crisis" showed that over a 22 year period since 1981 that the cost of a public four-year college education had increased by 202%. What is interesting, during the same period the Consumer Price Index had gone up only 80%. In Texas, the Texas Higher Education Coordinating Board officials said for Texas Public four year universities they have more than doubled in the past decade. A few Universities that went up in the last decade are University of Texas (130%); Texas A&M (111%); TSU (132%); and University of Houston (96%). Though these are Texas schools, the similar increases have incurred throughout the U.S. Private universities have not escaped this increase. Last decade they also grew over 42%. The U.S. Census Bureau, March 2002 found that on average, a person who receives a college education earns about 89% more than one who does not.

Benjamin Franklin once said "An investment in knowledge pays the best interest". John Hancock said "The only thing more costly than saving for college is not saving for college." It is estimated that if you have a new born that by the time they go to a four year college tuition will cost over $197,000. In the Annual Survey of Colleges of the College Board and Data Base 2004- 2005, a four- year private college education will cost of over $ 253,000. So you have a choice, either pray that your child receives an academic or other scholarship or grant or start saving for college today. How about winning the lottery, or even better yet, put your child and maybe you in debt for the rest of your life to pay off the cost of college. You can save nothing and at college time have nothing. Or, you can save along the way and have part or all of college paid for. The choice is yours. So how do you save for college? There are several ways to save: Coverdell education savings accounts, UGMAs (Uniform Gifts to Minors Act), UTMAs (Uniform Transfers to Minors Act), and Series EE Savings Bonds, personal savings, Section 529 plan and even life insurance policies. The best legacy you can leave to your children is a quality education. Our armed forces have a saying "Be all you can be". What a legacy to allow your children to have the opportunity of pursuing an area of study that will provide them with the tools and training to work toward their dreams and goals. Let's discuss a few.

529 Plans- These are plans that were created in 1996 by the Internal Revenue Code Section 529. This is a plan that is sponsored by the various states for a tax-deferred college savings. The plans were initially created to pay for tuition and fees only. The plan was created to complement prepaid tuition plans that many states had set up. Where a prepaid tuition plan guaranteed that if a lump sum or regular payment plan would pay for college tuition, the 529 plan could have the ability to invest in equities and have potential to earn more. Tuition and fees are approximately 19% of college costs and growing. Room, board, tuition and fees combined account now for about 89% of college costs. The plan allows for tax deferred growth. This means that any earnings will grow tax-deferred and will be reinvested. Over time, this can make a tremendous difference. In a study by T. Rowe Price Associates Inc. in 2005 they showed someone savings $5,000 a year for an 18 year period. They compared saving in a taxable vs. tax-deferred account. The funds that were saved tax-deferred were about 19% higher at the 18th year. Those extra dollars could make a tremendous difference in making sure that college is paid for. What I have done in the following chart, is pick a few different periods that someone starts saving in a 529 plan. I have used an 8% rate of return. This is amounts provided by John Hancock Freedom 529 plan. This is figures through their research will be needed when a child of that age goes to college. Of course, returns will vary depending of the performance of a 529 plan you pick. You will see, the longer you wait, the more you will have to put in to still have less at college time. If you can't save these amounts monthly, or annually, at least start saving. When planting a garden, if you plant seeds, over time they will grow into crops.

Child's Age	Amount Monthly	Amount Annually	Lump Sum	Estimated Value at College Time
1	$ 415	$ 4,813	$ 47,413	$ 197,092
5	537	6,217	53,069	162,148
10	850	9,844	61,096	127,047
15	2,181	25,271	70,337	99,545

The funds must be spent on qualified education costs. The qualified educational costs are room, board, tuition, and fees. Even computers have been allowed. Now the money can grow tax deferred and if you take it out for room, board, tuition, and fees, all the growth will come out income tax free. This allows the money that would have gone to taxes each year to stay in your account. It then allows it to earn money on the taxes each year until the funds are taken out. In a 529 plan, it has an owner which in most cases would be a parent, grandparent, or someone who is setting money aside for college for a beneficiary (child, grandchild, niece, nephew, or child of someone you know). You have the ability to have several 529 plans on a child. For example, if I could open up an account on my child, my wife could, her parents, my parents, anyone we could get to open an account on our child. Each 529 plan can contribute under current law $12,000 a year. There is the ability to make a contribution of $60,000 per account at the beginning. However, you would not be able to make a contribution for 5 years to that account. This option of $60,000 is per account and a good planning tool for a grandparent or parent that wants to provide for college. When you open the 529 account it is still an asset of yours and is included in your estate upon your passing. The child is a beneficiary. Of course, you will want to have a contingent owner in case of your passing prior to the child going to college.

The 529 plans are flexible. If you have a child that doesn't go to college, or acquires a scholarship and doesn't need the funds, you can change beneficiaries. You can change to yourself, spouse, another child, cousin, niece, or nephew. Grandparents who set up the plan can switch the beneficiary between grandchildren. You can set up your own plan if you are thinking about going back to college and then later switch it your children. In a 529 plan there is no earnings income limit on the ability to make a contribution.

Under current law, if you have funds left over, you will pay tax on the deferred growth that you take out and also be assessed a 10% penalty. The current law only offers the tax deferred benefits through 2010. There is strong feeling in the financial planning community that this date will be extended. However, when using this vehicle, this is something to take into consideration.

A question comes up quite often if you already have a custodial account, can you switch the funds to a 529 plan? The answer is yes. However, you must liquidate the funds where they are currently. If you have them in equities, you many have a capital gain or capital loss. This means, if you have a current capital gain, you would have to pay taxes on the gain in the year you made the switch. However, realize that when you transfer funds to the Section 529 plan, the future growth grows tax deferred. If you take it out for room, board, tuition, and fees- the growth will not be taxed.

Educational IRA (Coverdell Educational Savings Accounts) is another option to save for college. Annual contribution can be only $2,000 a year. Remember the Section 529 plan allows $12,000 per year. If you make more than $190,000 as a married couple, you are phased out to how much you can put in for the Coverdell. For anyone other than a married couple, the phase out is form $95,000 – $110,000. Qualified educational expense now includes elementary, middle and high school expenses as well as college. Contributions can be made up to the due date of the return including extensions.

If you get up a **UGMA account** (uniform gift to minors act), a parent would lose control over the money when the child reaches the age of majority at 18. You might have thought about an Ivy League school, but at that age they are thinking about that red shinny sports car. A section 529 plan is still owned by the person who set it up and they are still in control over the assets until the funds are distributed for room, board, tuition, and fees. When applying for financial aid, UGMA accounts are consider the students assets and approximately 35% is included in the formula to see what the student can qualify for financial aid. The 529 owned by another only includes about 5.6% in the financial aid calculation.

A unique way to save for taxes is a little tax planning tip I have for grandparents. Please, promise not to tell anybody. Well, here goes. Have the grandparent consider opening a Roth IRA. They must be in it for at least 5 years or age 59 ½ when they take the funds out and when they take the funds out, the earnings are income tax free. When your grandchild goes to college, you can pull the funds out and give them under current law $12,000 a year toward college. The funds will not be added in any calculation toward applying for financial assistance. By the way, a parent or other interested person (aunt, uncle, etc) could consider opening the Roth IRA.

When you child is in college, I often am asked about whether or not to give them credit cards. I have seen when a student is in their senior year of high school, they start getting applications for credit cards. You need to sit down with your child and discuss the responsibilities and obligations of having a credit card. You need for them to understand that they need to know how much they have charged and that balances need to be paid for. It is good to have a student get a credit card for college with restrictions and limits. There are cards that are called secured card. This is where funds are deposited with a bank and they can charge up to that amount. This type of card is good if you feel that your child will not be able to control their spending habits. Another thought is to get your child added to one of your credit cards. By doing this, you will get the monthly statement and will know what they are charging on the card. If you give a credit card to a child, you need to be clear about what the card is to be used for (books, tuition, groceries, rent, healthcare, school supplies, etc.).

Sometimes when we save for college we start saving late or with our current financial situation, we are unable to have enough to pay for college. That is when we have to turn to financial aid. Loans, grants, and jobs can bridge the gap to enable your child to have the experience and opportunities from a college education. No matter what financial situation you are in, I always recommend that you complete the standard financial aid forms. Colleges offer all types of assistance, merit-based and academic. I recently visited with a client who made too much by federal standards to get financial aid. He had a wife and three children, moderate income, and didn't live a high standard of living. His daughter got a merit based scholarship. In fact some universities give scholarships for out of state students who attend their colleges. If you get offers from more than one university, look to see if they have school rivalries. I remember one time when I suggested this to a client who had offers from both the University of Texas at Austin and Texas A&M. He told both that they had gotten offers from the other university. One of the Universities offered an additional $5,000. Guess where their child went to college? In my tidbit section, I have a few websites you might want to check out that might help you get scholarships. You need to be like a detective and when you child starts attending high school, start investigating varies ways of getting financial assistance. Talk to others who have children in college or about to attend and see what they are doing. Visit with your school counselor to get their advise. Contact your place of worship to see what recommendations and assistance they can give. Contact fraternal organizations you belong to and inquire about what programs they may have for financial aid. Go to bookstores and see any current books on scholarships or grants. One important point on scholarships, everyone goes after the large scholarships. I have recommended that you also go after the $500 and above scholarships. Not as many apply for the smaller scholarships and your chances increase when you apply.

In looking for loans, one source of loans is federal college loan program called Parent Plus or Grad Plus (formerly called PLUS (Parent Loan for Undergraduate Students)). Parents can borrow up to the cost of attendance less any other financial aid your child receives. Your child must be enrolled at least half-time, your dependent, and since July 1, 2006, applies to undergraduate, graduate and professional students. This loan is not a need based loan and is available anytime during the year. You can apply through the university or your local bank. The interest rate is adjusted yearly on July 1st is based on the Treasury-bill rate. Repayment starts 60 days after the funds are fully disbursed with a 10 year repayment term. You have the ability of consolidating the PLUS loans together, but not with Stafford or Perkins Loans. It is important to note that the loan is with the parent, not the student. You are responsible for payment, if your child makes a payment late, they still will look to you for payment. If the loan is denied, you may be eligible to increase the amount eligible for a Stafford Loan.

A Stafford Loan is for students and are either provided by private lenders (Federal Family Education Loan Program (FFELP) or by Direct Lending Schools (Federal Direct Student Loan Program(FDSLP)) . Stafford Loans are either **subsidized** (the government pays the interest while you're in school) or **unsubsidized** (you pay all the interest, although you can have the payments deferred until after graduation). As of July 1, 2007, Stafford Loans allow dependent undergraduates to borrow up to $3,500 their freshman year (up from $2,625), $4,500 their sophomore year (up from $3,500) and $5,500 for each remaining year (independent students and students whose parents have been turned down for a PLUS loan can borrow an additional unsubsidized $4,000 the first two years and $5,000 the remaining years). Graduate students can borrow $20,500 per year (up from $18,500), although only $8,500 of that is subsidized. There are also cumulative limits of $23,000 for an undergraduate education and a $65,500 combined limit for undergraduate and graduate. (For independent students and for students whose parents were denied a PLUS loan the cumulative limits are $46,000 and $138,500, respectively. Some medical school students may be able to borrow up to $40,500 a year (up from $38,500) and $189,125 total.) Repayment begins six months after the student graduates or drops below half-time enrollment. The standard repayment term is 10 years. To apply for a Stafford Loan, you must submit the Free Application for Federal Student Aid (FAFSA). Even though the unsubsidized Stafford Loan is available to all students regardless of financial need, you must still submit the FASFA to be eligible. You can receive a subsidized loan and an unsubsidized loan for the same period.

Another loan you might consider is the **Perkins Loan** which is awarded to undergraduate and graduate students with exceptional financial need. This is a campus-based loan program, with the school acting as the lender. Many feel that since it is a subsidized loan and the interest is paid by the federal government during your child attending college and 9-months after, it is the best loan available. The interest rate is lower and also has the 10-year repayment period. The amount of the loan set by the school's financial aid office with limit of $4,000 per year for undergraduate students and $6,000 per year for graduate students, with cumulative limits of $20,000 for undergraduate loans and $40,000 for undergraduate and graduate loans combined.

When you are assessed for financial assistance, controlling what is shown as your income from the year prior to your child going to college is critical. For example, if your child starts college September 2008, your 2007 tax return will be looked at. It is important that you try to hold down your income that year. For example, if you have a bonus or stock options you can take, you might delay taking them until 2008. If you are self employed, you might delay sending out invoices at the end of the year to help lower the current year taxable income.

Checking out the various Universities your student attends is also important. Check with the universities about their freshman visitation programs. They usually have orientations about the university where parents and students can come visit. They talk about a host of different things from applying to the University, housing, campus tours, financial aid, and more. You might also consider visiting colleges on the Web. Many universities now have virtual tours, giving all types of information. So go to www.campustours.com.

CHAPTER Eight
Scared to be in the Market

I can start quoting a lot of statistics how over time the stock market has provided an average investor more than letting their money sit at a bank. I want you to understand, that letting your money sit at a bank also has risk. If your returns do not keep up with inflation, you have purchasing power risk. With inflation, the products you purchase and the services you pay for cost more in the future. Yes there will be periods that the market moves up and there will be periods that the market will decline. Cato the Elder once said "patience is the greats of all virtues". No one knows when the market will go up and when the market goes down. There is a lot of statistics that show that it is important to stay in the market. Movements in the market usually have a major impact over a short period of time. If you are out of the market when the market rises, you have lost that opportunity cost of gains. So how is one way to help hedge for the average investor. It is called dollar cost averaging. Let's use an example. John decides that he wants to save $100 a month in mutual funds. So he invests in ABC mutual fund when the shares were $10 a unit. He got 10 units. Now wouldn't it be your luck that as soon as you start investing the market went down. Let's look at the following chart. John even though the market was declining still invested his $100 a month. He got more units when the market declined and fewer units when it rose. After this 6 month period the value of the unit in this example was only what it was when he started investing. John didn't know when he started to invest when the market for his investment was at a high or at a low. But with dollar cost averaging, at the end of 6 months, in this example, he had a $127.70 gain. That came out to a 21.28% gain. The return of course for any investment will vary depending on the market conditions at that time. However, with dollar cost averaging, an investor first has the ability of investing smaller amounts on an ongoing basis. The investor stays in the market and has the opportunity of capitalizing when the market makes the upward movements.

Month	Amount Invested	Cost per Unit	Number Units Purchased
1	$ 100	$ 10	10
2	100	8	12.5
3	100	6	16.66
4	100	8	12.5
5	100	9	11.11
6	100	10	10
Total	600	8.24	72.77

CHAPTER Nine
Procrastination

I know I need to put money away; I will get to it soon. I just need to pay off a few bills and then I will start. Sound like some excuses you have heard. I will give you a hint; most people will have bills all their life. If they wait to pay them off, only additional new bills will start. You may delay, but time will not. (Benjamin Franklin) In a moment of decision, the best thing you can do is the right thing to do. The worst thing you can do is nothing. (Theodore Roosevelt) Procrastination is the fear of success. People procrastinate because they are afraid of the success that they know will result if they move ahead now. "Because success is heavy, carries a responsibility with it, it is much easier to procrastinate and live on the "someday I'll" philosophy." (Denis Waitley).

Procrastination has tremendous financial cost to you and your family. The longer you wait, the less you will have for your various life events. The Social Security Administration in 2003 stated that Social Security and pension accounts will account for only **39%** of the income needed at retirement. The remainder will need to come from personal savings and investments you have made. Do you want to work a lifetime to end up living at a lower lifestyle in what is to be your golden years?

If you are not already aware, let me teach you the Rule of 72. Albert Einstein came up with this theory. He said it was the 8th wonder of the world. Of course, the Astrodome in Houston hadn't been built yet. You basically take 72 and divide it by the interest you earn. This will tell you how long it will take for $ 1 to grow to $ 2. Like playing horseshoes, this is close and not an exact number. So let's take a 4% return, it will take about 18 years for your money to double. At 6%, it will take 12 years. At 8%, it will take 9 years and at 10% return, it will take about 7.2 years. Here if you procrastinate, you are losing the doubling effect of your money being invested. Two big questions I have to ask you. First, what is an average return you will feel comfortable earning until you retire? Second, how many doubles will you have of your money? Remember that money not being spent on toys when a child is born. Let's say you invested $1,000 at an average 8% return. At age 9 the money invested would grow to $2,000 and at age 18, the money would have grown to $4,000. What if you had waited until your child was 9 to start saving. That $1,000 invested that year would only grow to $2,000. Big difference. But what if someone was 21 and had a chance to put away into a 401K plan at work or an IRA $1,000. That is 44 years from age 21 to age 65. At the 8% sample return, every 9 years the money would double. Let's see, $1,000 would grow to $2,000, $4,000, $8,000, $16,000, and about $32,000 at age 65. I guess I can sum up by saying that procrastination will cause you to loose the opportunity to have sufficient funds and quality of life for the various life events you want. I started with a quote in this book and I think it is good to restate it here "The greatest discovery of my generation is that human beings can alter their lives by simply altering their state of mind" Psychologist William James. You need to make a decision here and now that you will not procrastinate when it comes to your financial affairs. That you will take action, be decisive, and go forward, Will there be some mistakes along the way? Most likely. Will there be some times you may not listen and put funds in the wrong places? Probably. But you must persevere and not procrastinate. You have already shown a strong commitment of improving where you are financially by picking up this book, working on the exercises in this book. As Nike would say, "just do it."

CHAPTER Ten
Going for the Gold

You have heard it over and over; my neighbor and my best friend say that investing in real estate right now is the only way to go. In fact, gold is hot, no foreign investments are hot, no etc, etc, etc. Have you ever been told not to put all your eggs in one basket? It was a sad day in Houston during October, 2005 when Astroworld closed down. I remember growing up as a child going on the rides with my family and friends. But I remember how exciting it was to go on the roller coaster. It was such a thrill to start climbing up the coaster. You could hear the chains pulling you up. You had that adrenaline going and the feeling of excitement as it climbed. Then all of a sudden you saw the top. You weren't sure what was going to happen. You wanted to stay on but part of you wanted you to stop. Then, fate hit you and down you went. You could hear the screams of those riding. You felt the force on you as you descended to the grown. Many would want to get off, yet they are not sure when and how. It was interesting to observe now that you rose slowly to the top and you descended at a much greater speed.

What if you had put all your money in real estate and the bubble exploded in your area and real estate values declined in a hurry? What if gold prices fell, foreign investments declined? What if you had all your apples in one basket? Those historically that invest in only one segment of the market may have rapid gains, but their losses may far exceed their gains.

Now comes up the benefits of diversification of your investments. Morningstar Associates, LLC in 2004 did a study of a 20 year period from January 1, 1985 through December 31, 2004. They took an investor who invested $10,000. They looked at three different approaches:

Contrarian Approach – Invest the $10,000 using the worst-performing category of the prior year.
Bandwagon Approach – Invest in the best-performing category of the prior year.
Diversified Approach – Invest equally among the nine multiple equity styles.

Human nature is most investors would want to take the bandwagon approach, that is, invest is what was the best-performing category of the prior year. Here was the interesting result. Had you invested using the Contrarian Approach – you would have at the end of the 20 year period $496,432. By using the Bandwagon Approach – you would have at the end of the 20 year period $557,113. Interesting, the one that performed the best was the Diversified Approach. This approach at the end of 20 years would have yielded $689,114. That's about 38.81% higher return than the Contrarian Approach and about 23.69% higher than the Bandwagon Approach. So, have I made a good case for not putting all your eggs in one basket?

I also want to make a case for realizing that past performance is no indication of future performance. This does not mean that performance from a particular investment will be repeated in the future. There are cycles where various investment styles will have similar opportunities for growth in the future. It is amazing to see that most people make investment decision on the past performance of an investment. Just because a particular investment made a lot of money in the past doesn't mean that it will continue the same course in the future. I am sure that you have heard of the Morningstar ratings. A 5 star rating is the best and a 1 star rating is the worst. Morningstar is historical data; they rate on what an investment has done in the past.

The financial research corporation did a study from January 1, 2005 – April 30, 2005. They looked at investors in mutual funds. They looked at the net cash flow to funds. The net cash flow is the net between funds being added to a fund and the funds being withdrawn from a fund. This study goal was to see where the investors were putting their money. They looked at the funds with a Morningstar rating of 4 and 5 and found that during this period about 124 billion more was taken in these funds than investors withdrew from these funds. They then took the 1, 2, and 3 star Morningstar rated funds and found that they had a negative 51 billion cash flow for this period. It is human nature that we want to believe that the past performance will be indicative of what the future performance will be. Human nature (a little fear and greed) will make us lean this direction. However, it is the time in the market with diversification that usually wins over timing the market.

CHAPTER Eleven
Stay the Course

I am sure that at some time you have watched a sporting event and your favorite team may be down. You wonder what is the coach thinking and why he keeps doing what he is doing. Then the third and fourth quarter comes and slowly your teams point spread gets closer and closer. Two minute warning, five seconds, one second, they won. Oh my goodness, it is a miracle. You might think your team got lucky, or just maybe, the team had a plan. They had a long term objective of how they were going to play the game. They stayed focused, they stayed on course.

A lot of investors try to time the market. Listen carefully and reread what I am saying. It is not the timing of the market, but the time in the market that will count long term. A mere day or two out of the market can make a huge difference in your return. Smart investors don't risk missing the biggest single-day gains. If you pull out of the game and sit on the sidelines, you don't know when to get back in the game.

A study by the FactSet Research Systems, Inc for the period December 31, 1994 to December 31, 2004 showed that if you had invested $10,000 in the S&P 500 Index, you would have had an average annual total return of 12.07%. But you used emotion in investing and during that 10 year period you **missed the 10 best days**. You reduced your average annual return to 6.89%. What if you missed the **20 best days**, your return would have dropped to 2.98%. If you missed the **30 best days**, you would have a net annual average return of -.039%. That's right; you would have lost money during that 10 year period. A simple 10, 20, 30 days can make a tremendous difference over a 10 year period. As I have said earlier, past performance can't guarantee future performance. The lesson here is you have to ask yourself why you are investing? Are you investing for the short term(less than 2 years), midterm (2 to 7 years), or for the long term (over 7 years). Even though the market has ups and downs, you need to realize the following when the market it down. By putting your money on the sidelines while you wait for the market to recover, you lose the upswings in the market. Human nature is you are going to wait to see the market rising and feel comfortable before you get back in the market. Meanwhile, you have lost the opportunity to participate in the upward movement of the market. Recently I had a client that got nervous and he called me. We went over his portfolio and he reiterated that he didn't need the funds in this particular part of his portfolio for another 8 years. Yet, the market had moved downward about 5% and all he could think about was the period during 1999, 2000, and September 11th. He listened to a neighbor who quite often lost in his positions in the market and moved his investment to a fixed vehicle. Within a period of less than a month, the market had rebounded and he still was in the fixed vehicle. By not focusing on his long term objects, his plan, his needs, he lost in the rebound in the market. Remember as I said earlier; whenever you think about getting out of the market, always ask the following question. Why are you investing? What are these funds for? By moving the money are you staying focused on your long term objectives? Stay focused and consider staying the course.

CHAPTER Twelve
Cost of Inflation

Over time the cost of inflation makes our future dollars worth less. If we don't save enough for retirement, our spending power will diminish. Since 1914, inflation has averaged around 3.1%. Over the last 30 years, it is less than 5%. So let's use an average between the two and take 4% for an example on inflation. What if you have $1,000 today and you want to buy something in the future, let's see what $1,000 will buy in the future. Let's look at the chart below and see what time and inflation does to the value of our money.

Years from today	Assume Inflation Rate is 4% - what $1,000 would buy in today's dollars
5	$ 822
10	675
15	555
20	456
25	375
30	308
35	253

Below, I have a chart showing how inflation has changed each year from 1914 to the present. You will see that it goes up and down; there is no steady increase each year. In the chart above, you will see that after 20 years a $1,000 in the future will only buy what about $456 buys today. So to say it another way, you will need a little over $2 in the future in 20 years to buy what $1 buys today. This is where most Americans fall way short. They think of retirement and future life events in today's dollars. They forget to add inflation to the growth in amount that they will need in the future. This applies to all life events, future home, college, weddings, second homes, and retirement. It is better to have a larger savings than what you need in the future. So are living off of $50,000 today, and you are 20 years from retirement, plan to have at least $100,000 that you will need to draw to provide similar living standards. You may hear people say you only need 70% of what you live off today in retirement. This is something that should be relative to what your particular living standards are. What life style do you see yourself having when you retire? Retirees today are more active than our parents and their financial needs are much greater. Remember the exercise you did at the beginning of this book where in 5 year increments you listed how you saw your retirement. What you were doing, places you were going, family and friends you may help financially. In a recent article AARP did a study and around 40% of those they surveyed said that they were spending more in retirement than they spent while they were working. Plan ahead, plan for increase in annual cash flow needs, don't miss the boat.

Inflation Statistics

YEAR	Annual Inflation
2006	3.24%
2005	3.39%
2004	2.68%
2003	2.27%
2002	1.59%
2001	2.83%
2000	3.38%
1999	2.19%
1998	1.55%
1997	2.34%
1996	2.93%
1995	2.81%
1994	2.61%
1993	2.96%
1992	3.03%
1991	4.25%
1990	5.39%
1989	4.83%
1988	4.08%
1987	3.66%
1986	1.91%
1985	3.55%
1984	4.30%

1983	3.22%
1982	6.16%
1981	10.35%
1980	13.58%
1979	11.22%
1978	7.62%
1977	6.50%
1976	5.75%
1975	9.20%
1974	11.03%
1973	6.16%
1972	3.27%
1971	4.30%
1970	5.84%
1969	5.46%
1968	4.27%
1967	2.78%
1966	3.01%
1965	1.59%
1964	1.28%
1963	1.24%
1962	1.20%
1961	1.07%
1960	1.46%
1959	1.01%
1958	2.73%
1957	3.34%
1956	1.52%
1955	-0.28%
1954	0.32%
1953	0.82%
1952	2.29%
1951	7.88%
1950	1.09%
1949	-0.95%

Year	Rate
1948	7.74%
1947	14.65%
1946	8.43%
1945	2.27%
1944	1.64%
1943	6.00%
1942	10.97%
1941	5.11%
1940	0.73%
1939	-1.30%
1938	-2.01%
1937	3.73%
1936	1.04%
1935	2.56%
1934	3.51%
1933	-5.09%
1932	-10.30%
1931	-8.94%
1930	-2.66%
1929	0.00%
1928	-1.15%
1927	-1.92%
1926	0.94%
1925	2.44%
1924	0.45%
1923	1.80%
1922	-6.10
1921	-10.85%
1920	15.90%
1919	15.31%
1918	17.26%
1917	17.80%
1916	7.64%
1915	0.92%
1914	1.35%

CHAPTER Thirteen
Emergency fund - vs. Savings

It is a hot summer day and you go outside to start your car. You look at the dashboard and there you see that it is 100 degrees in the shade. You turn on the engine, crank up the A/C, and in a few minutes it will be 72 degrees in the car. You start the car and all that comes out of the vents is hot air. So you get your car checked and you get the bad news- that it will cost $750 plus tax to fix the A/C in your car. There are only another 90 days left until the cold weather comes. You can wait or then again, is this one of those emergencies that you will get the credit card out to get the A/C fixed. What if the A/C went out in your home? How about one of your children gets hurt, you have to pay the deductible on your insurance ($250, $500, $1,000). Of course, you could ask the doctor if you could leave your child there for two weeks until you get paid. Here are just a few examples of why you need to set money aside for emergencies. How much, the costs are relative to the lifestyle you live, the home you have, and the toys that you get. For an average middle class family, I recommend at least $2,500.00 for the average family. You don't have that now, ok, start saving some money each pay period. Put it in what I call near money or safe money. Put it in an account at a bank (preferably a money market account). You want to be able to take this money out at a moments notice without any type of risk of loss of principle (any fluctuation in the stock market). If you put this in a mutual fund for example, you would run the risk of needing the money when the market is down.

Now comes how much should you have in savings? For the average American family I recommend three to six months of living expenses. What if you, your spouse, or significant other lost their job, how will you pay for your living expenses? What if you became disabled? So what if you receive disability insurance, there may be a waiting period before it starts. Also, your spouse or significant other may have to take time off from work without pay to help care for you. You need to have savings set aside to replace the loss of that paycheck for a period of time. You still will have your household expenses, note payments, and all your monthly expenses to pay. Paying late can affect your credit and living off credit card can put you and your family into added financial pressures. The best thing that could happen is that you force yourself to have more money for your retirement years and you didn't need any money for emergencies and savings.

Savings goes well beyond my example here. Remember at the beginning of this book, you wrote a draft of what you saw your life plan. What events and activities you projected would happen for you and your family. Some were short term (within two years), some were mid term (two to seven years) and the remainder long term (over seven years). Where and how you save is important in funding the various life events. To illustrate, let's assume that you had a bad cut on your hand. You can stop the bleeding and leave it alone. If you do that, could it get infected, and cause you to possible loose your hand or create more severe complications? The same principal is with our money. If we set money aside for savings and in emergencies or saving for an event we have to take the funds out before the investment matures or the market is up, we can loose our principal. So we want to have different buckets of our money. Remember the story of Goldie Locks and the three bears. There was three bowls of porage. In investing, we have three bowls of investment, short term, mid term, and long term. We want to have the ability and opportunity of picking where we take funds from when we need funds for different life events. If you have all your funds in one segment of the market, you could have good news and bad news when you take the funds out. Your good news is that segment is at its high and you have taken out funds at the right time. The bad news could come when the segment of the market you take the funds out of are on the decline, at their low, or at the beginning of a growth mode. You want to have safe money so that if you take money out in the short term, it will not be impacted by the downturns in the market to avoid loosing principle. So now you may see the reason why I had you draft a life plan earlier in this book with the number of years before the activity or event would occur. This would help you plan on how the funds would be invested and be available at the time you needed the money.

$2,100. Most people unfortunately spend first, before they save first for retirement and other life events. We are the richest country in the world, but the worst savers. The savings rate in the United States is only around 3%. Highlighted by fewer and fewer companies offering retirement plans, we must now set as a priority to take a more active role in retirement savings. You can no longer take for granted that a company and the government will provide for us in retirement. So why do we fail at savings for retirement. First and foremost, most of us don't have a plan of attack of how we will save. This is made even worst by most of us only being taught a trade or profession. They teach us how to earn money, but most of us are not taught what to do with our money. This lack of knowledge, along with the affects of taxes and inflation, poor investment selections, doom many Americans. We need to start a systematic savings plan and make sure that we do not procrastinate.

Health and daily sustenance are two big expenditures during retirement. To begin with, I would like to tell you the rule of 219. If you take a married couple who spends $5 each per meal, three meals a day, in twenty years from age 65 – 85 they will spend $219,000 on food. To top that off, it is estimated that during the same 20 years, the average couple will spend approximately $238,000 on healthcare cost. Healthcare costs increase during retirement and becomes a large expenditure to most Americans. I have heard and seen many seniors that can't afford their medicines. I have seen and heard about their missing pills to help stretch the days they take a prescription. Don't let this happen to you. Plan, set goals, **plan**, review goals, **plan**, and keep the process going!

CHAPTER Fourteen
Will you be able to Retire?

Most people if you ask them that question, will side step the issue. The reality is they don't know. Most want to use the 9 digits that they use in their social security number. Social Security, when created by Franklin D Roosevelt, was only created to be a supplement. In fact, at that time, most American's were to begin receiving payments after their estimated life expectancy. Anna Mae Fuller, the first recipient, had only made one payment and did quite well on her investment. Most of us won't be that fortunate. You have heard the stories that Social Security won't be around when we retire. Currently, the average recipient will get under $ 1,000 a month. Tell me, what quality of life will you derive if you only get Social Security when you retire? The most someone will get monthly today is a little over

would happen for you and your family. Some were short term (within two years), some were mid term (two to seven years) and the remainder long term (over seven years). Where and how you save is important in funding the various life events. To illustrate, let's assume that you had a bad cut on your hand. You can stop the bleeding and leave it alone. If you do that, could it get infected, and cause you to possible loose your hand or create more severe complications? The same principal is with our money. If we set money aside for savings and in emergencies or saving for an event we have to take the funds out before the investment matures or the market is up, we can loose our principal. So we want to have different buckets of our money. Remember the story of Goldie Locks and the three bears. There was three bowls of porage. In investing, we have three bowls of investment, short term, mid term, and long term. We want to have the ability and opportunity of picking where we take funds from when we need funds for different life events. If you have all your funds in one segment of the market, you could have good news and bad news when you take the funds out. Your good news is that segment is at its high and you have taken out funds at the right time. The bad news could come when the segment of the market you take the funds out of are on the decline, at their low, or at the beginning of a growth mode. You want to have safe money so that if you take money out in the short term, it will not be impacted by the downturns in the market to avoid loosing principle. So now you may see the reason why I had you draft a life plan earlier in this book with the number of years before the activity or event would occur. This would help you plan on how the funds would be invested and be available at the time you needed the money.

CHAPTER Fifteen
So you're not married

Today more and more couples are living together who are not married. There are interesting and unique considerations that you must consider with your financial affairs. Sure one of you may pay the rent, the other groceries or other bills. You might just open up an account together and put all your funds in jointly. You are in love and want to share your life with the other partner. Maybe you are not at a stage to consider your relationship long term. There are short term considerations that are very important to consider.

First, of all, I like to call it risk management. You might have homeowner's insurance, renter's insurance, or car insurance. You need to check with your insurance agent to see about the coverage you have. You might say, Ed, I have coverage on my residence. True, but you need to read between the lines in your policy. What if you had a fire? Your insurance policy could treat the one of you as what is know as a "houseguest" Your policy might have a limit on the houseguest to stay in your home, (i.e. several weeks, month…) If the person is there longer, the provisions of the policy may cause their staying in the home to void the insurance policy. Wait, they didn't tell me. Did you ask the insurance agent before you bought the policy? Did you have them show you where it is in the policy? Ignorance of the fine lines is not an excuse. Rule no. 1: when you are living with anyone who you are not legally married with, "Any type of insurance I have I need to ask if we both will be covered." Also, get it in writing. Is this a growing concern? In 2000, when the census was taken, they estimated that around 11 million Americans were living together.

Health insurance and disability insurance is a must for Americans to have. You will need to have separate coverage. Then comes what happens with the passing of a partner? Have you discussed what the beneficiary designation is on any life policy? Do you have a will? What provisions have you made for the other partner? How about those joint bank accounts, brokerage accounts, and investments. For bank accounts, have you set up what is known as a POD (Payable on Death)? This is a provision that you can set up with your account at your bank that at the passing of a partner, the funds will immediately transfer to the other partner. Let's face it; they will be grieving over your passing. Do you want to add the extra problem of potential challenges by relatives and possible other interested parties to tie up the funds in those accounts. After all, they will have to still pay the car notes, house note or rent, groceries, and other monthly bills. You don't want to tie the funds up. Now, for those that have a joint securities account, you want to call you brokerage house, mutual fund company and make sure that you have a TOD (transfer on death). This way the joint funds can automatically go to the surviving partner. All these tips sound great, to do, but it will only work if you make this a priority to call today or tomorrow to have this set up on any accounts you want to go to your partner. This can be huge issue that most non-married couples do not take care of.

You may have heard before where there is a will, there is a way. In this case, a will enables you to have your way of leaving your legacy you have built to who you want to. If you die without a will, each state will impose their rules on specific rules. You may have assets that you have accumulated together or just assets you want to leave to your partner. Make life simpler on them and without all the fighting and legal hassles by creating a will. In your will be explicit who you leave your assets to. For example, what if you both have a house you own. You may have bought it together or may have owned it before they began cohabitating with you. Do you want them to potentially get kicked out of the home by children or other interested parties?

So take time, go through all your assets and if there are beneficiary designations, check to see who is listed. You can ask the institution where you have funds (i.e. banks, savings & loans, life insurance, brokerage accounts, annuities to send you change of beneficiary forms if you want to change someone's name). If you really care about your partner you are cohabitating with and want them to have particular assets, show your love by taking action and make these changes. Do they have a birthday coming up, anniversary, or the holidays? What better gift than to get your financial affairs in order.

CHAPTER Sixteen
Secret Agents

    Slowly out of the fog in a trench coat there you stand. You look to the left, you look to the right, you look over your shoulder, and you continue to walk. Slowly you are no longer visible in the fog. You carry in your briefcase some of your valuable papers. No one knows the combination to your briefcase. No one else knows where the multitude of financial papers, legal documents, and other important papers are. You see, you are secret agent! You have worked hard all your life, you through diligence and some luck have accumulated the wealth that you have acquired. Whether it is $10,000, $50,000, $100,000, $500,000, $1,000,000 or more you feel like it is billions of dollars. No way are you going to let anyone know how much you have. Then in the fog along the journey of life, you are struck with an illness, you become disabled. Maybe you loose your speech, become unable to communicate with any one. Over in the corner of your bed stand your loving spouse, your beautiful children, and those friends and relatives that are so close to you. They care so much for you. They wish they could have expressed just how much they feel about you. In your position as a secret agent, you thought you were saving the world. You thought that you were a great provider for your family. But in your current state, you have left your family in a tremendous mess. You see, they don't know what the family has financially. They don't know where the accounts are. They don't know in your secret hiding places where you have put all your valuable papers. You in fact, have done one thing; you have left one tremendous mess. You have left your financial affairs in such a state that they may not have access to funds. They may take days, weeks, and months to find all that you have secretly earned. They may have to take the precious dollars that you have worked so hard to accumulate and earn and needlessly spend in on financial advisers, legal advisers to help clean up your secret mess. So, how do you feel as that secret agent? Can you envision and see what your family has gone through. Or, are you the innocent loving spouse who will go through not only the emotions of your love one's illness or passing, but the trauma of dealing with the fear, and worry of your finances. Let alone the job of searching and finding where everything is.

It doesn't stop here. What if instead of being hurt, your life ends. Those that you care so much about and provided for all your life are left not only grieving, but put at their wits end where do they go from here. What did you leave them? Where are the funds and how can they get access to them? I have had many people over my career call while they were in the state of shock grieving from the loss of a loved one, crying because they don't know where to go from here. They may walk into your study, but just the thought of going through all your papers is overwhelming to them. They don't know how you filed your papers or where you have kept your records. You see, you were the one who maybe paid all the bills. You were the one that made all the investments. You wanted them to feel safe and secure and not worry about money. You also may not have wanted to let them know how much you had for the fear of them overspending. Your list can go on and your secret ways can far exceed what you are doing to your loved ones.

So wake up, you are not Secret Agent! You are a hard-working American that has been fortunate to have accumulated some wealth to pass on to your family. To be able to make sure that funds are there for your loving spouse. To leave a legacy for your children, family members, or charitable endeavors. But you are putting them through a lot extra grief. So how can you change it? First of all, do you trust your family? If so, why not have recorded in one place a document that you can give instructions to your family of specific things you want them to do upon a disability or your final days here on earth. A document recording where you have valuable papers, who your advisors are, what burial instructions , pall bearers, maybe what you want to be remembered by, specific items you would like members of the family to have, and just whatever you want your family to know. Is this a legal document to hold up in court? NO, I am not an attorney. But is it letting your family know about where, when, how, and why with your financial affairs and other things important to you.

I remember once in my accounting practice a client of mine was late to an appointment for her taxes. She had just come back from Massachusetts after her grandmother had died. In her hand was a bonsai plant. When she was a little girl her grandmother had bought the plant. They spent many hours as she grew up pruning the plant, sharing their days, and sharing their lives. Yet she was crying when she came in. Trying to comfort her, I remember her telling me how her sisters had fought with her when she was there for a week. After the funeral, they went to her grandmother's home. They were the three beneficiaries of her grandmother estate. Her sisters had been to the home already and miracle of miracle, most of her grandmother's jewelry was gone. Other heirlooms and items were no longer in the house. When she went to the house, she sat in the sunroom where the bonsai plant was. She immediately picked it up and put it by the front door. One of her sisters accused her of taking items from her grandmother's home. It had no real monetary value, but it had just a sentimental value …….priceless!!!!!!!!!

The first thing I can suggest is make sure you have a current valid will. I am a strong believer of not doing a do it yourself will. Going to office supply house to get a form to insert the blanks or copy it from some other source may leave out important provisions that can cause conflict and extra legal costs after your passing. The form may not take into consideration specific laws of your state and have up to date provisions. If you want specific things to go to members of the family, it's your life, your assets, and you're right to state where you want items to go. So what if you add another several pages to your will. You will limit conflict amongst your loved ones. I can't tell you how many stories and times I have heard people fighting over pianos, pictures, jewelry, furniture, etc. I know an attorney that suggested and had in the will each family member was given fake money of $1,000,000 to be used at an auction. They had the attorney or someone the attorney picks; meet with all the beneficiaries at the individual's home. They then bid on the items in the house. After a few ridiculous amounts paid for some items, everyone got a reality check that when they spent the $1,000,000 in fake money, they no longer would inherit any items. The family had a two hour break and sat down and decided what they really wanted. Items started going for $1.00. The games, the fighting, the childlessness stopped when they saw what they would eventually loose out on. The decedent was truly a wise man. But you can save your family from all of this by putting it in your will. Or, instruct in the Letter of Love, where you want different things to go if you didn't put it in your will. Again, the Letter of Love is not a legal document, but only a guide to let your family know where you have your assets. It also gives your wishes you want to convey to your family. Is this a perfect solution? No, but it I have found it has been a tremendous help. So, as the chapters of your life continue to grow and change, so be the Letter of Love. Add, subtract, delete, and voice your wishes. It's your life. It's what you have created, it's your legacy. Let all that are close to you know what you wanted, not what they wanted. Of course, the best binding course of action is to put what items and to whom are to be distributed in your will. Let your family watch the television show Family Feud and not be a reality show of family feuding. Life is to short.

CHAPTER Seventeen
Managed Money

Oh, I can do it myself. I am the pro, what is so hard about investing my money? After all, I have friends at work that give me good tips. I invest with emotion, fear, and greed. I went to college, wasn't taught how to invest my money, so what? Sound like someone you know, a friend, co-worker, or for some, yourself. Yes, we can do a lot of things ourselves, tax returns, plumbing, home repair, etc. But I think most of you agree that we usually go to someone who is trained in that area to make sure that it is done correctly. It may cost a few dollars for their services, but you utilize their talents to make sure the job is done right. They give us benefits and a return on our investment higher most of the time than if we did it ourselves.

Most Americans enjoy sports. If you analyze a team the

owners and management hire a coach. Their job is to put together a team of professionals to create a group that their goal is to perform above average and be the best they can be. If a professional does not perform up to standards, they are replaced with another professional. They are trained to perform in the best and worst of times. Many times they go out and perform even with injuries. Their coach is there to keep them on track and put together a winning lineup. If a member of the team is not performing up to standards, they are replaced at a moments notice. It doesn't matter how much they cherish their relationship or if the professional has Hall of Fame potential. Past performance was yesterday and what their performance is today and how they perform today, and expected in the future based on their health and other factors becomes what is focused on. They take the emotion out of the situation. No matter what others are saying, they stay focused to the teams plan. Their may be times when they are up and times when they are down. Take for example in 2005 when the Astros were down at mid season about 15 games. Their coach Garner stayed focused, had a plan, no matter what locally and nationally people was saying they held tight, stayed on track, and weathered a bad period. They analyze and review the current situation. Based on what they see happening at the moment, they know how situations have worked in the past. They have studied their opponents and know detailed statistics on their past, recent, and projected future performance.

Anyone can put a team together. But a few questions, will it be the right mix? Will you end up having too many players in one spot? Will you become overweighed in one position and weak in another? Will you have fear and greed in making your decisions? Are you starting to see the big picture? With professional Money Managers you now have a team of professionals. They have brought together professionals experienced and knowledgeable in the various segments of the market. They review your tolerance for risk and based on passed trends, data, current events, social, and economic forecasts, they build a portfolio for you. They do not invest with emotion. They invest with a plan with your objectives, and risk tolerance. They look at how that segment is performing today and based on current market conditions, how it is expected to perform in the future. They don't keep an investment because of emotion. I can't count how many times I have heard from a client, my deceased spouse or my parent had money in this company and they said it was a great company. I should keep my money there. So what if markets change, the stock is falling, it is a good company. Times change, needs for companies change, and if you are not in the right place at the right time, you loose. Technology constantly changes and the products and services that company provides may be replaced by newer and younger companies. The legacy that you have inherited from your love ones may slowly die away. The money manager, like a coach, puts the team of professionals together. They constantly meet and analyze where they currently stand. They review information about the various investments they had made on your behalf. They may call the various companies and get more data. They review trends, historical cycles in the market. They keep a hands on approach to where the market is today, what current events are happening that may impact where the market direction is happening. They know that along the way their will be spikes in the market going up and going down. They will hold and sell based on the strengths and weakness of the companies they invest in. They will have one eye on the rear view mirror, what has happened in the past. But they will have the other eye on where the economy is today and where it is expected to go in the future.

How are Money Managers compensated you might ask? Most are compensated on a fee bases. That is, they get a fixed percentage of the money under management. Let's say for example that they get $100,000 to invest for you. If their fee was 1% for example, they annually will receive $1,000. They have a vested interest in your success. If the value of your portfolio goes up, their fee grows. If it goes down, their fee decreases. In most cases even with their fee, the net yield to you is higher. For those of you in business have you ever heard the saying "to make money, you may have to spend money." I know, you don't want to pay a fee. Ever been in a mutual fund? Who do you think is paying a fee? You have professional money managers working for the mutual fund company investing your money for a fee. If you invest by yourself, you could be exposing yourself to too much risk in one area of the market.

Let's take one of Ed's examples. Imagine, you own a house on the golf course and your home is behind the green. At the back of your house, you have a great room that has a giant window. Just your luck, someone slices the ball and travels guess where, in your window pane. If you had the one big pane, you now will have risk and exposure and have lost the whole window pane. Now instead, let's make a tic tac toe board out of your window pane. You now have nine panes of glass instead of the one big pane. Now when the ball hits, one pane breaks. Your exposure is minimized and your risk of loss has been reduced.

By using the analogy of the 9 panes in a tic tac toe board, an investor has multiple equity styles that they can pick from for their investments. Let's look at the following chart:

Large-Cap Value	Large-Cap Core	Large-Cap Growth
Mid-Cap Value	Mid-Cap Core	Mid-Cap Growth
Small-Cap Value	Small-Cap Core	Small-Cap Growth

Let's also think of it another way. When you were growing up you probably had at one time in your life played on a see-saw. When you and your friend were at the end, one end was up while the other end was down. When one end went down, the other came up. That is what happens with the different equity styles. They may not equally move, but several of the styles move in different directions.

Most investors when they invest by themselves tend to sell after the market has dropped significantly. Quite often they will wait too long to buy when the market has come back. If an investor doesn't have a disciplined plan, and stay up with where the market is and indicators for upward movement, they will be rewarded by low returns. In the Third Edition, of 'Winning the Loser's Game", by Charles D Ellis, he found that for the period of 15 years (1982-1997) an average mutual fund earned about a 15% annual return. A typical mutual fund investor on the other hand, only averaged about 10%. Why a difference? Most investors invest with fear and greed and do not establish a long-term investing program. They jump around from one investment to another and don't stay on course with their investment strategy. Most chase past performances. You may have heard disclaimers from financial investments that "Past performance is not indicative of future performance". Of course, we want to believe that we have found a winner and like when we were growing up, don't want to always listen.

Another area that is important for investors to understand is what is called style-drift. Quite often an investor will invest with different mutual fund companies, stocks, bonds and there will be overlap of holdings in a particular equity style. Remember that roller coaster at Astroworld. You enjoy the ride up, but you hate the ride down. By utilizing professionals they help keep you on course. They remove the emotion from investing. They make sure that you do not have too much holdings in one segment of the market. They rebalance portfolio's to keep a good asset mix.

How do you find a money manager? You usually go through a stock broker or through a financial planner like me. Many advisors will set minimum size accounts they will take on. Likewise, some of the money managers also have minimums. In a majority of the cases, a smaller amount invested will yield a higher management fee. As you invest at different levels, there will be price breaks in the management fees that are charged. Some will charge a quarter ahead and some will charge in arrears (at the end of a quarter). In most cases, you do not commit to long periods that your funds have to be invested. You have the ability of taking your funds out when you want to..

CHAPTER Eighteen
Investing

An investment in knowledge always pays the best interest - Benjamin Franklin

Good investments, bad investments, how do you know the difference? When someone has not saved any money, they will most likely have uncertainty of what to invest in. Let's face it, you see on the news the stock market going up and going down each day. No one wants to lose money. You want to do better than what you are making at the bank, but what do you invest in. A common question is " Is the stock market to risky for someone to invest in?" First, you have to ask yourself why you are investing. Is it for the short term, mid term, or long term? Too many individuals are like sheep and they follow the herd. Quite often it is so easy to follow the herd and react to news in the world instead of acting on opportunities. Knowing what to do in different situations come from both experience and also from working with professionals that are experienced in the market. Be careful when picking advisors that they have experience. Quite often I have seen someone go with someone working at a company that has a big name. Just because the company has a big name does not mean that the individual advisor you are working with is qualified to assist you with your needs. The Financial Planning Association, which I am a proud member of, has a list on their website of questions to ask a planner. If you have an opportunity I would check out their website.

When you make an investment, I would like to make a suggestion. I would like for you to write down when you make a particular investment why you made that investment. Was it to have money for an emergency, savings, rainy day, a new home, college, retirement, or some other life event? Then when the market changes, and you are considering selling that investment, I want you to revisit why you made that investment. Most people don't realize that if you get out of an investment within one year, you have around a 30% chance of loosing money. But as time periods increase, 5 years, 10 years, and then 15 years, the statistics for losing money drop to where an investment of around 15 years you have a high probability that you will not loose your principal. Without boring you with statistics, stay focused on the reason why you made the investment. This is worth repeating, someone who tries to time the market does not have a crystal ball. You work on two key elements of fear and greed. We simply attempt to be fearful when others are greedy and to be greedy only when others are fearful (Warren Buffett). Many times you may not have the experience or the tools to help you evaluate the current market to make a good decision. Historically, approximately 1.9% of the time has money been made by timing the market. On the other hand, about 91.9% of the time money has been made by time in the market. It is not just a play on words. History repeats itself, cycles repeat themselves and long term there is an upward trend in the market.

When investing in the stock market, you are investing in companies. What mix of companies you have at different cycles in the market can make a tremendous difference. You might have thought that if the market goes down you may loose all your money. So many individual's invest blindly in companies. They may invest by reading periodicals talking about certain stocks or mutual funds that have done well recently. Realize one important point, that is yesterday's news and may not reflect today or tomorrow. Take a sports team that has done well in the first part of the season. How often do they perform well for the whole season and become the number one team for that year? How often does the same team stay number one for the next season? In many of these publications when you see them talking about particular companies or mutual funds, look and see if by some chance these companies are advertising in the publication. Could that be a coincidence or just maybe…(I know you were smart)

You must also understand that you shouldn't invest by what others are saying. I have had potential clients and clients come in and tell me about stocks that they have invested in because a friend or someone at work had given them a hot tip. Then, wouldn't you know it, some excuse or reason was why the stock went down. My old rule of thumb, "if they were so good at investing in stocks, how come they haven't given up their day job?".

Let's look at investing in the market another way to reduce some of your fears. Let's say you have been asleep and your alarm clock just went off. Who manufactured your alarm clock? You turned it off, got up, turned the lights on and went to your restroom. You used more utilities in the rest room, when you washed your face, and took a shower. What utility company did you use? You went to the kitchen and had something for breakfast. Maybe you had juice, milk, coffee, etc. What companies sold those products. You finished getting ready for work and put on your work clothes. What department store did you get them from and what manufacture made your clothes and shoes? You turned on your alarm, went to your driveway and turned the engine on your car. A few days ago you filled up your gas tank. Maybe going to work you stopped somewhere to get a cup of coffee. Do you do these activities when the economy is up, down, and sideways?

Population of the country grows and you and your fellow Americans use these services each and every day. As the population grows, more and more individuals need these products and services. And most of these products and services most likely are from public companies. Companies that issue stock and you either can buy individually or through 401K plans, etc. So, does this change your perspective in investing in the stock market? As Warren Buffet said, "Why not invest your assets in the companies you really like? As Mae West said, "Too much of a good thing can be wonderful".

One of the first places that you invest is in your retirement account at work. One common plan is the 401k plan. In a large portion of plans an employer may have the provision to match on what you put away 50% on the first 6% that you put away. So, let's see what that really means. Let's say for a round number that someone makes $10,000 a year in salary. If you put away 6%, you are putting away $600 a year, or $50 a month. But that also means that your employer will pay you additional income year of 3% or another $300 per $10,000 of salary a year. That comes out to a 50% return on your investment and the best part, you made that the first day that you put the money away. Also, by you putting away the 6% or $600 in this example, you have lowered your taxable income for the current year. So, let's say that you are in the 25% tax bracket, on $600 reduction in your taxable income, you have now lowered your income tax obligation for this year by $150. To break this down to a dollar, for every dollar you put into your 401K, you are putting in 75 cents if you are in the 25% tax bracket, the other 25 cents is coming from your current year savings in income tax. So let's see, invest 75 cents, save 25 cents in tax, make a 33 1/3% return on your money you put away. But it doesn't stop there, what if your company matched 50% on your first 6%. Isn't that another 50 cents being set aside for your retirement. So if I am adding right, someone in the 25% tax bracket will save 25 cents in tax, plus get another 50 cents that is matched by their employer in this example. So they have 75 cents and they also had put in 75 cents. So, in reality, you have made 100% return on your money and you haven't even had time for the money to be invested yet. So a question, if you haven't already invested in your 401K, doesn't this give you a reason to do so?

To be a smart investor you have to have a disciplined approach. You have probably heard the saying "it's the time in the market, not timing the market.". You have to understand the cycle of emotion. The six step financial planning approached I mentioned earlier in the book is I feel the best approach for the average American. You need to add to this approach, a team of professionals to guide you along the maze of your financial future. As you approach different stages of your life you will see different roads to follow. An experienced team of professionals have seen you situation many times before and with their years of experience, can guide you through which road to take to help you meet your personal goals and objectives for you and your family. Sure you can do anything on your own, but I thought I would share with you an interesting study done by Dalbar, Inc. During the period 1986 – 2005 they studied the returns of the market and the returns of the equity mutual fund investor. During this time period, the S&P 500 index averaged a 11.9% return. During that same time frame, the average equity fund investor only averaged a 3.9% return. That is a 8% difference. Many choose to do it alone and they usually bought high and sold low and yielded a lower return than what the market performed.

With an analogy of a baseball team. You should be the owner (investor). You need to find a general manager to run your team (investment advisor). He will find the right head coach for you (portfolio strategist). The head coach then will find, hire, and monitor the performance of the players (investment managers). If they are not performing, he will bench them or if he feels it is right, he will replace them.

Saving for retirement can never start to early and is only to late when you are gone. The earlier you start, the more opportunities you have. Where to put your funds, depends on a variety of things.

Life is full of uncertainties. Future investment earnings and interest and inflation rates are not known to anybody. However, I can guarantee you one thing.. those who put an investment program in place will have a lot more money when they come to retire than those who never get around to it. (Noel Whittaker)

CHAPTER Nineteen
Risk

Twenty years from now you will be more disappointed by the things you didn't do than by the ones you did do. So throw off the bowlines. Sail away from the safe harbor. Catch the trade winds in your sails. Explore. Dream. Discover. (Mark Twain)

When you invest, there is an element that has us feeling vulnerable, uncertain, and has a thread to our principal, RISK. Risk has a direct relationship to the return on your investment. As a rule of thumb, the higher your return, the greater the risk you have of losing part of your principal. More conservative returns on the other hand reduce your risk. A combination of your goals, time horizon, inflation, and taxes have an impact on the risk that you may take in your investments. When you invest in the stock market in stocks and bonds, they have a higher degree of risk than investing at a bank that has the FDIC insurance.

The FDIC, Federal Deposit Insurance Corporation is an agency inside the US Government. This is insurance that is backed by the full faith and credit of the US Government. When a bank that has FDIC Insurance should fail, it is insured dollar for dollar on the principal and accrued interest up to the basic insurance limit of $100,000 per insured account. If someone has an Individual Retirement Account (IRA), they are insured up to $250,000 per depositor per FDIC insured bank. It is important to note that there are a number of banks that also sell mutual funds, stocks, bonds, annuities, municipal securities, and insurance policies. When you invest in these items, they are **not covered** by the FDIC Insurance. The contents of your safety depot box are also not insured. This is important to know. So many times I have had new clients come to my office for planning and they feel that since they have invested through their bank that all their money is insured up to $100,000. The type of ownership you have can increase the amount of funds that are covered by the FDIC Insurance. If you have a single account in your name both for example in a checking account and Certificate of Deposit (CD) at the same bank, you wil have to add both together. If there combined balance is over $100,000, you are only covered up to $100,000.

The same combined account concept goes for retirement accounts. Let's say you have the different type of IRA accounts (Traditional, Roth, SEP IRA, Simple IRA, Keogh, Section 457). Reminder the combined value of these accounts are insured up to $250,000. If you have more than $250,000, these funds do not have the protection of the FDIC insurance. When you are married, if each of you has an account in your individual name, you will each be covered for $100,000 or a combined total of $200,000. When opening accounts at a bank, you might have several beneficiaries that you would like to leave money to upon your demise. You can up what is known Payable-on-death (POD) accounts. These accounts are revocable trusts and have also been known as Totten Trust or testamentary accounts. This type of accounts is more complicated and you should do a little homework before you set them up. If you have multiple beneficiaries and you have funds over the FDIC insurance limit of $100,000, you should open up multiple accounts with a separate beneficiary on each account. This is an area that too many rely on heresay. The FDIC has a website www.fdic.gov that explains more and has calculator for coverage. It is always better to get it from the correct source than rather than someone who may not understand all the facts. One last point, FDIC charges an insurance premium to banks that have the FDIC coverage. The actual dollars the FDIC has is less than 2 cents per dollar. If there is a run on banks, in reality, there will not be dollar for dollar coverage. The likelihood is slim, but you should not have a false sense of security.

There are several types of risk that I wanted to address.

Market risk – the movement of stocks and bonds based on the current market environment. They may move up or down and usually moves over a shorter period of time of less than a year. Think about it, if you don't sell the stock or bond, your investment has the opportunity of recouping any decline in value and have the opportunity of yielding you a higher return on your investment.

Inflation risk – This is the risk of the cost of inflation increasing more than the growth of your investment over time. Let's say that you had inflation of 4% for the year. If what you have invested your money in earned less than 4%, you are in the hole. Even though your account has a higher balance, it did not keep up with the increase cost for the items we consume. By investing too conservative, "you run the risk that most of us don't think about."

Purchasing Power Risk – When you bought a car, didn't you want to know what the drive out sticker price is with all the fees and charges? The same goes for what our actual prurchasing power is on an invest. That is what return we got, less inflation, and less any taxes we paid on the earnings we made. That truly is the net effective yield. The more that we can invest tax deferred and tax advantaged, the more compounding and growth we make on our investment.

Longevity Risk – This is when someone outlives their income. With medical technology today, we are living longer. We need to stretch the live of our investments. By investing too conservative, we run this risk.

Timing Risk – This is a two edge sword. This risk is that we invest funds at the time that the market is at a high. The second side of the sword is that luck would have it- you will need the funds at a time when the market has gone down. That is why we need to have funds available at different time periods, i.e. short term, mid term, and long term. If we need to utilize funds, we can pick it from investments that we aren't forced to take out of when that particular investment may be down.

Global Risk - Not only what happens across country, but what happens around the world gives us a larger risk of movement and yields on our investment.

There are more risks we could discuss, but my point here is that literally anywhere we invest our money, there is some form of risk. Being too conservative can have risks to us as much as being to aggressive. There is no security on this earth. Only opportunity (Douglas Macarthur).

Security is mostly a superstition. It does not exist in nature, nor do the children of men as a whole experience it. Avoiding danger is no safer in the long run than outright exposure. Life is either a daring adventure or nothing (Helen Keller).

CHAPTER Twenty
Retirement

Another good thing about being poor is that when you are seventy your children will not have declared you legally insane in order to gain control of your estate.
Woody Allen

In your lifetime, most of us have had several jobs. The real reason we work is to create the lifestyle we want to live. This lifestyle also means we want to have a quality life during your retirement years. So I ask another question, have you ever put down on paper what you feel you will need to have monthly when you retire? We all have heard numbers like you only need 70% when you retire. Now the real figure, you need to first define what you will be doing during retirement. You will need to take into consideration expenses that were benefits paid for by previous employers. A married couple from 65 to 85 are projected to spend an estimated $238,000 out of pocket for medical costs. Inflation increases the cost of items we consume and we tend to underestimate our needs during retirement. Do you remember the rule of 72 I shared earlier? Let's say that inflation is 4%. Take 72 and divide it by 4, you will get 18. If you feel you need to live off of $50,000 a year in today's dollars for retirement, what will you need when you retire? IF you are 18 years away from retirement and inflation has averaged 4% (in reality, it is around 3.1%), you will need $100,000 18 years from now to have the same purchasing power that you can buy with $50,000 today. We must now focus on making sure you have enough money to meet your future needs. When you retire, you swap a paycheck for a withdrawal check. This withdrawal check comes from several sources. It could be a retirement account from a previous employer. It might be a fixed payment for the rest of our life or it could increase based on inflation. For most of us, this is not enough. We might also get funds from social security. When social security was set up , it was only a supplement. Too many individuals feel that they can live off their social security check (false). Lower income Americans receive around 78% of their income from Social Security, while higher income receive around 24% of the income in retirement from Social Security. Tomorrow's retirees, if they want their aged years to be golden, will need to rely more on earnings, pensions and other retirement plans (EBRI Issue Brief No. 289, Employee Benefit Research Institute, January 2006).

From the 2006 National Summit on Retirement Savings, the following was shared:

Retirement security has become a national priority. A quick look at the overall picture shows why:

- Nearly one-third (33%) of American employees work for employers who do not sponsor a retirement plan (EBRI Issue Brief No. 289, Employee Benefit Research Institute, January 2006)
- Nearly half (49%) of American workers do not participate in an employment-based retirement Plan (EBRI Issue Brief No. 289, Employee Benefit Research Institute, January 2006.)
- Employees today shoulder a larger burden of risk and responsibility for their retirement savings, as more and more employers shift from defined benefit plans to defined contribution plans.
- Many Americans will not be able to maintain their pre-retirement standard of living with their current rate of saving toward retirement.

So with the American dream our parents and grandparents had of working for a corporation and they would give us the benefits we need in our retirement years, it now comes down to one very important realization, you can only count on **you**. You need to prioritize the funds needed to be set aside for your retirement. How is America doing as a whole? The personal savings rate is very low. After holding steady at 7-11% from 1960 to the early 1990s, America's personal savings rate—the percentage of personal disposable income not spent on personal outlays—has fallen in the last seven years to levels not seen since the Great Depression, and was negative at the close of 2005. (News Release: Personal Income and Outlays," Bureau of Economic Analysis, U.S. Department of News Release: Personal Income and Outlays," Bureau of Economic Analysis, U.S. Department of Commerce, January 30, 2006Commerce, January 30, 2006)

I hear from new clients coming in that their parents and

grandparents did not live to be very old. They did not live in the environment we live today. They have too short a term thinking and don't plan for longer life expectancies. U.S. life expectancy are growing and statistics that a married couple age 65 has a chance that one of the spouses has a 50% of living to 92.

So many questions come up in planning for retirement that we could write a whole book on just this topic. But a key concept to understand is that how fast you deplete your funds will have a major impact on how long your funds will last during retirement. Do you want to make sure that there are funds still left to help support a spouse or significant other? Do you want to leave a legacy to your children, other family members, and charities?

My rule of thumb is that you don't want to take out more than 4% of your assets annually. You have a very strong chance that you will not run out of money. Key point here is how much money will you need. Let's use an example of a couple I just saw. In their particular situation, they will need about $100,000 a year to maintain the lifestyle they want to live. They will get $30,000 from Social Security and Retirement Accounts, so they will need to get $70,000 annually from monies they have set aside for retirement. So how much money should be their target? If your took $70,000 and divide it by 4%, they will need to have at least $1,750,000. In this example, even with cost of inflation, they will have funds to last at least 30 years.

So how much do they have to save annually? There are many variables here. First of all, how many years before retirement, how much have they saved so far, and what expected rate of return do you anticipate you are going to make? In my website www.planningaheadwithed.com, I have calculators that you can put this information in and it will tell you how much you need to save monthly to meet your goal. It is better to understate your rate of return to be on the conservative side that to not save enough for retirement. Ok, so what if you can't save all that you need to. You got to start somewhere and like taking baby steps, you got to crawl before you walk. As you start saving, you can always increase the amount you set aside each and every month. As my rule of thumb, if you are in your 20's, you want to save at least 10% of what you make annually. For your 30's, at least 15%, 40's at least 20%. Make a rule, save before you spend. You will thank me later.

When to retire is always a hard question for a lot of us. You really need to sit down before you retire and put on paper what you see your lifestyle like in retirement. Are you going to be a home body? Are you going to wake up, spend all day reading the newspaper? Or, are you going to be the type that will play golf, tennis, or other sports a few times a week. Go to exercise class, play cards with friends, travel, and more. All these activities require money that you will need to have when you retire. You need to put down on paper your costs for your lifestyle. You also need to ask yourself before you retire, what will you miss the most when you stop working? Will you still feel useful and productive? What priorities do you have now with the rest of your life? I have seen active individuals get depressed and feel like they have no self worth anymore. It has caused some of us to have a sense of loss of self esteem. This has brought on controlling attitudes, being irritable, and leading to a disaster of the marriage by ending in divorce. A sense of purpose during retirement for those of you who have been active is critical. You may want to keep social networks with those in your industry and at work. Part time work in your area or expertise or volunteering with you companies might be a bridge to retirement. Even if you don't need the funds, keeping yourself mentally active and still having a sense of worth may keep you from having your health dwindle due to lack of activity. You might say you want to work with charities by volunteering, travel, go back to college, or spend time with your grandchildren. As funny as this may sound, maybe do some of this before your retire. See if this is activities you really want to pursue. Quite often I have found that after someone does these activities for a short period of time, they get bored, or really find that is something they don't want to do. You have an active life while you work, you need to also have an active life when you retire.

In the years of counseling couples about retirement, I recommend that both retire at the same time. You both will have the same issues in retirement and will have more compassion on how to deal with it with the other spouse. Your chores may change (my favorite, taking the trash out). You still need to be aware and respectiveful of your spouses needs. Sit down and discuss how they see retirement. When you schedule events, keep a calendar and as you did when you got married, remember the word "We". I have seen individuals when they go into retirement feel that they worked hard all their lives, they are now going to do the things they want. Yes, that is important. But like anything else, done in moderation. A healthy retirement means not only staying physically active, but emotionally and supportive to your spouse or significant other.

One last point, if you have been independent during your marriage, you need to still have independence. I remember one Sunday for a half hour everywhere my wife went, I went. She kept saying "What are you doing?" I said "I am practicing for retirement". And her reply, "You are never retiring". You need to set activities that you both will do together and independently. Both of you have your friends as a couple and individually. You need to develop your own interests. If you haven't had hobbies for years, prior to retirement you need to really sit down and think about what you want to do. You need to start these activities prior to retirement. Don't think about them, then try them, get bored, and then have nothing to do. It is not only important to have funds to support you both during retirement, but enjoy your retirement and be happy.

Where you live makes a difference. There are seven states currently that have no state income taxes – Alaska, Florida, Nevada, South Dakota, Texas, Washington and Wyoming. If you plan or moving when you retire, state taxes can help you deplete your funds faster. For example, rates in California are as much as 9% and rates in Illinois is as low of 3%. When you move to a state that has state income tax, look at what is taxed, (your retirement income and social security). Property taxes and sales taxes need to also be looked at when you move to another state. You also need to see what taxes in the state you move to is on both estate and inheritance taxes.

CHAPTER Twenty-One
Taxes

I am proud to be paying taxes in the United States. The only thing is – I could be just as proud for half the money — Arthur Godfrey

To me, the last three letters in theirs is the IRS. We earn it, they tax it. We spend it, they tax it. We die, they tax it. Do you see something in common? We can pay taxes now, pay taxes later, and there are some legal ways to never pay taxes. As I told a client once, if I told you the later, I'd have to kill you (just kidding). Making investments is not our only concern with what we make, but how much of the return we made we have to give back to the government in taxes. In making investment decisions during our lifetime with tax considerations as part of our selection process, will contribute to what we have when we retire.

Paying taxes now vary on a variety of investments in vehicles at banks, savings & loans, dividends on stocks, and capital gains. With dividends, you need to look at companies that might pay qualified dividend distributions and those that might pay capital gains dividend distributions. Both have a more favored tax rate than ordinary dividends and interest. When holding a stock, you need to know that the holding period is important. If you hold a stock less than a year, when you report any gain you will be taxed at the highest tax bracket your level of income is in. If you hold the stock over a year, you will be taxed under current tax rules at 15%. If you are in the 5% and 15% tax bracket, the tax rate on long term capital gains (held over a year) are taxed at a lower bracket.

Paying taxes later are in tax deferred vehicles like annuities, and retirement accounts. Let's assume in this example that you have $10. You make a 10% return on your money, or make a $1 profit. If you are in the 25% tax bracket, you have to give 25 cents of your profit to the government. In reality, you only made 75 cents, or a net yield of 7.5%. At the beginning of year two, would you rather have $10.75 or $11.00 to invest?. That extra amount, the 25 cents can now help you earn future returns and give you more funds at retirement, or work for you when you need the money for a future event. So tax deferred vehicles like an annuity help you accumulate more dollars for retirement. Note, they are tax deferred. When you take the funds out at a later date, you will pay taxes on the earnings at whatever tax bracket you are in at that time. Annuities have special features as they first are issued by insurance companies. They may have a feature that they protect the principal at a future date. When you invest in the market, you run the risk of the market going up or down and there is always a chance that the value could be less than the principal you have put in. Annuities can pay fixed rates (fixed annuities) or they can have subaccounts that are invested in the market (variable annuities). Like buying a car, annuities have different options and features that you can add to your annuity contract. Some features may have guaranteed payments for your lifetime, etc. You need to be aware of the various options, look at your situation, and analyze what is the best for you. A financial advisor can help you here. Just make sure with what annuity you are being shown that the individual sharing the annuity with you doesn't just represent one company. You want that advisor to bring you to the market place and not just to one company. Annuities have other benefits, and different states have different rules. But let's look at Texas. Annuities are judgment proof, creditor proof, and bankruptcy proof. These additional features add extra value in picking this investment vehicle. That is why it is so crucial to invest the time in education so that you can be informed and you have a better chance of making smarter investment decisions. It also is critical to build of a team of advisors like myself you have years of training, education, and hands on experience to guide your through the maze of investments, taxes, and life time goals.

Another vehicle to pay taxes later is your retirement accounts (i.e. 401(k), 457, 403(b), IRA's, SEP-IRA'S, ROTH IRA'S, etc.). You are putting funds away now and saving taxes on them. The amounts that would have gone to taxes also grow and have the opportunity to grow in the future.

Both however, will have penalties if you take out before age 59 ½. If you take the funds out early, you not only will pay taxes at the tax bracket the funds put your income in, but you will be slapped on the wrist with a 10% penalty for early withdrawal. There are exceptions for disability and death. In 401(k), if you are a first time homebuyer, you can take out $10,000 and not pay the 10% penalty. But always, when you take out money of a retirement account, you will pay taxes on the amount you took out at the current tax bracket these funds put you in. See, the government either gets you now or later. If you earn income now, you pay taxes. If you are able to put it in a vehicle that is tax deferred, they will tax you when you take it out. If the money grew, you will have a bigger pile of money. You also will have more money that will be subject to taxes down the road.

On your retirement account, when you are age 70 ½, you must start taking out funds. In recent years, the IRS is tracking this much closer. See, if you don't take out the required amount (known as RMD's – required minimum distributions), the IRS can assess a 50% penalty on the amount that should have been withdrawn. They have tables for you to use. Please note that you look at the balance in all your retirement accounts at December 31, (the year before your required distribution). For example, if I hit 70 ½ in 2008, I would have to look at my retirement account balances at December 31, 2007. Let's assume the balance was $ 272,000 at December 31, 2007. If I am 70 ½ and the factor is 27.2. I would have to take out a minimum of $272,000/27.2 or $10,000. There is a special rule under current law for someone who has hit 70 ½. You can elect not to take a distribution that year. Instead, you can delay withdrawing funds until next year. But the next year you would have to take out twice, once before April 1st and the final before year end. What is it important to review this. Look at what taxable income you will have when you reach 70 ½ and what income you will have the next year..

Paying taxes never. Yes, believe it or not, there are a few legal investments. First , is tax free municipal bonds.

Usually you will have a lower yield on these investments. So when you analyze these investments, look at what an equivalent taxable yield would be. Let's assume you make 4% tax free and that you are in the 25% tax bracket. You would take 4% and divide it by .75% (1- tax bracket (25%)) and get 5.33%. So a yield of 5.33% in the 25% tax bracket would net you 4%. When looking at tax free municipals, also look at other elements of your tax return. If you are receiving social security, you may have income that will make your social security taxable. If you are single and you have income of $25,000, 50% of the excess income of social security is taxable. If married, the current figure is $32,000. When you make over $44,000 married (or $32,000 single), 85% of social security becomes table above this amount. If you can keep your taxable income below these thresholds, you will enable part or all of social security not to be taxed increasing your net effective yields. So annuities (tax deferred vehicles) and tax free municipals could become important tax planning vehicles.

Life insurance products have what is known as the inside build up. You have not only the death protection benefit, but you have an account that is growing. There are different type of accounts but the important concept her on insurance products other than term insurance allow this account to grow tax deferred and the ability to take funds out during your lifetime tax free via loans. Upon your passing, the death proceeds are reduced by any loans and the remaining balance goes to your beneficiaries income tax free. Depending on who owns the policy, the funds may not be included in your estate for estate tax purposes and avoid any potential estate taxes.

Some tax considerations to review, in investing in mutual funds, learn when the mutual fund company pays out their dividends each year. You don't want to buy into a mutual fund at the end of the year and shortly after they issue dividends on the account. Your account shows taxable income to you with no increase in value. I remember in 2000 when a new client invested in October, showed a dividend that they had to pay tax on in December, and the account went down 5% by year end. They were not what I call a "happy camper". The same goes for a sale of a mutual fund. You don't want to get a dividend issued on a fund and then sale it a day or two later. That also would show extra income to you. It is always a good idea to keep your statements on mutual funds so that you can accurately keep your tax basis in your investment. You might over the course of years change brokerage accounts where you hold that mutual fund. You might transfer the account to the new brokerage account, but the cost basis information may not be given to the new brokerage firm. Usually the last statement of the year will have a detail for the year in a mutual fund and you can keep that statement instead of each month. Just check to make sure that statement does in fact have the information before you discard the interim monthly statements. And as always, any financial data you discard, shred.

When selling stock, reminder to look at whether you have held it over 1 year . The tax rates are lower over a year. But don't just keep a stock for tax rate. If you feel that it has reached a high and is moving downward, look at the economics of selling now or holding the stock. If you sell a stock at a loss and want to buy it back, you must wait more than 30 days before you buy it back. If you buy it back in 30 days or less, the loss you had recognized will be considered a wash sale and you will not be able to take the loss on your tax return.

Year end planning and review of what gains you have can make a difference. Think of two bowls of porage. You put your short term gains and losses in one bowl. In the other bowl you put your long term gains and losses. You net each bowl. If you have losses in either bowl (short or long term), you can now net any loss against any net gain in the other bowl. If you have excess loss, you can take $3,000 on your tax return and the remaining loss gets carried forward to future years. If you have both short term and long term losses, you always use short term losses first. Let's say it's the beginning of December. You look and see that you have a good year with stocks and have net gain of $20,000. You now can look at your existing portfolio and see that there are two stocks that have a loss of $5,000. Tax planning would suggest that you make a sale of these stocks to recognize the loss of $5,000 in the current year and then have a net income of $15,000. Again, you must wait more than 30 days to buy the stocks back if you want to still have them in your portfolio. And of course, only sell the stocks if you feel that they probably will not recoup the loss.

Maybe you have a stock or mutual fund that has appreciated in value. You also have a favorite charity or place of worship that you want to make a donation. What should you do? Should you sell the stock and then give the proceeds to the charity or just give the stock to the charity? Let's see. If you sell the stock and have a gain, you will have to pay taxes on the gain. Then you will have to take the net proceeds available to give to the charity. You might have to take funds from other sources to give the total amount you wanted to give to charity. Something better, give the stock to charity. You will get to write off the full amount if you are under your charity giving limit for year and save on the taxes you would have to pay.

The hardest thing in the world to understand is the income tax. – Albert Einstein

CHAPTER Twenty-Two
Documents

We live in a society of paper. Some of us have too much paperwork, but some of the paperwork is needed. There are some crucial documents that you might want to have prepared. You can always prepare documents yourself by going to the web or buying them from a do-it-yourself service. Are the documents current with your all federal and state laws? Will the provisions apply to the state you are living in? Do you understand what you have signed ? So I would encourage you to spend a few dollars and hire legal counsel who is experience in the area you are seeking help in. If you are working with a planner like myself, they may be able to refer you to professionals who can help you. Now for some basis documents to consider.

What if you take ill? Do you remember the soap opera

that played out on television about Terri Schiavo where her family was at odds about her health care. To solve the problem, be proactive and you decide what you want if you take ill. You should prepare what is known as an **Advanced Directive**. This legal document states how you want to be treated should you become very ill and your chance of recovery is slim. This document goes by various names and needs different wording for various states. An advanced directive usually has two forms, one being what is called a Living Will. This legal document establishes the kind of health care you want or don't want based under various circumstances. You need not be vague and be specific. Address all types of medical care, custodial care, and end-of-life planning. The second form is what is called a Health Care Proxy (also known as a durable health care power of attorney). This legal document will allow you to name someone to act on your behalf and make health care decisions when you become incapacitated. After these documents are prepared, they need to be put in an accessible location. You don't want to hide them in your house and not tell anyone where they are . The individual you name to act in your behalf needs to have ready access to these documents.

Power of Attorney - This legal document will allow you to appoint someone as your agent engage in a variety of financial matters for you. You can limit the power of attorney to one activity or give them full authority. Quite often individuals are mislead in thinking that there is a one size fit all power of attorney. You usually create a power of attorney to act in your behalf if you become incapacitated. It is important that the power of attorney you create is a "durable" power of attorney. This allows the power of attorney to still be in effect upon your incapacity. For those of you who do not have long term care insurance, your durable power of attorney should also allow your POA to place your assets in trust to enable them to plan for government programs.

Your last wishes- don't let your last wishes go with you to your grave, make sure you have them written down somewhere for all to know. Your family is not in the best frame of mind upon your passing and this will also help them when they are grieving over your loss. At the same time, let them know where you have your important legal documents. They need to be readily assessable to your family. An example of some of the documents are: will, directives, power of attorney, birth certificate, deeds to your property, insurance policies, cemetery deeds, appraisals, retirement accounts, annuities, notes or liens you own. You also should have in your list the various credit cards you have, who they are with, account numbers, pins, and phone number of credit card company. It might be a good idea to make copies and give them to your spouse or whoever will become the executor of your estate. Tell them where you have a list of your assets. In this list of assets, be sure to include the location of assets and all their information (account number, who the investment is with, advisor on account, password or pin). If you have cash hidden at home, be sure to let them know the location. List the name, address, email and phone numbers of your advisors (attorney, cpa, insurance agent, broker, financial planner). Some items to consider:

- What are your last wishes for your funeral? Cover items of pallbearer, music, type of casket, ceremony, eulogizer.
- Where do you want to be buried? Do you have a burial plot? Where is it located?
- Where would you like your funeral service to take

place? What clergy would you like to officiate?
- If you have a pet, who do you want to take care of them. There are Pet Trusts you can set up. See info in Tidbits.
- If you served in the military provide information of your service number, branch, rank, and discharge date. This information is needed for your beneficiaries to check on any benefits that you might be eligible for.

Your Will - Only about 40% of Americans take the time to create a will. This legal document allows you to establish how you want your financial assets to be distributed among your demise. There are differences amongst the various states in the US and it is important that you make sure what is written will apply where you live at the time of your passing. With more and more of us having blended families, his children, your children, and our children we can't take for granted how assets will be distributed. If you don't create a will, then upon your passing, the state you live in may distribute assets differently that what you intended them to be distributed. There is so many variables that you just need to know that a will needs to be prepared the correct way. Some states may not accept a handwritten will. There are requirements for witnesses and again, each state has various rules. Word to the wise, get a professional to help you prepare your will. Go to an attorney and get it done right.

CHAPTER Twenty-Three
Insurance

We insure our car, we insure our house, however many of us do not insure our lives. Why should you buy life insurance? One simple answer, to provide a lifestyle for the living. It is not for you, it is for those who you provide care for. If you have children and a spouse, you want them if you have an early passing to have a similar lifestyle they currently have while you were still alive. Your death you know will cause emotional strains to your family. Does your death need to also create financial strains? Picking insurance is not always the easiest decision. You basically have two options, term life and permanent life insurance.

Term life does not have a savings component like permanent life does. Term is the less expensive cost of the two types. Term insurance is for a specified period of time. If you death occurs during that specified period of time, you are covered. Once that period is gone, the policy expires. You can get what is known as level term. The policy will be in force for a specified period of time at a specified premium. If it is guaranteed level term, the price will remain constant. If it is not guaranteed level term, the cost during the term could go up.

Permanent Life has a savings feature. Part of the premium you pay goes for the insurance coverage and the remainder goes for a savings feature known as "cash value." Most permanent life insurance has surrender periods whereby you are charged a surrender charge for getting out over a specific period of time. When looking at policy illustrations of a policy, be sure to look at what surrender charges are. During your lifetime, you have the ability to borrow out funds. I have seen this used for funding college, and supplement cash flow during retirement. At your death, the face amount of the insurance policy is reduced by any loans and accrued interest and the balance is sent to your beneficiaries income tax free. If you own the insurance policy, the face amount is included in your taxable estate.

The biggest question I get from my clients is "How much insurance do I need?" There are a number of variables, but to help simplify it, you need to consider the following:

- What are your final expenses (funeral, medical, probate, estate taxes)?
- What are you existing debts (credit cards, auto loan, mortgage, property taxes, and other loans)?

Insurance quite often is used to help retire debt your family has. But insurance also needs to help you with their future income needs. What if you were married and your spouse was home taking care of your young children? Even if they get a job now, there will be additional costs in having someone take care of your children. The job your spouse may get may not be able to bring in as much as you were earning. So you need replacement income to still take care of your families annual income needs. You need not only look at the shortfall in income, but still have funds available for college tuition, childcare, and emergencies. Even though there are a number of methods, I use the following method to keep it simple. After reviewing the above, you come up with an amount needed annually to take care of your family. Take that amount and divide it by 4%. So for example, let's say your family needs $40,000 annually after your death. If you take $40,000 and divide it by 4%, you get $1,000,000 in assets you need. You can look at what other assets you may have (cash, savings, securities, retirement accounts, current life insurance, real estate) and see where you are short. One thought about retirement accounts. They are for retirement, so consider making the calculation without the value of your retirement accounts when you have young children. Leave those funds to be used by your surviving spouse for their retirement. Another element to consider is that inflation has an impact on future costs for your family. By using the simple calculation above, you have not allowed for inflation effect on your cash flow needs. You might ask why I used 4%. There are a number of studies that if you only take out about 4% annually, you have a strong chance of not outliving your money. This is only true depending on your investments and net yields of your investments. So, in the example above, if you needed $1,000,000 and had $200,000 in other assets, I would recommend a minimum of $ 800,000 in coverage.

What about coverage on your spouse? Even if there is a

stay at home mom, you should still consider coverage on your spouse. Upon their death, you will need to have someone watch your children, help take them to all their social activities while you are working. You will still need to have funds for college and as I said earlier today, for a newborn it is estimated to be nearly $200,000 to pay for 4 years of college at a state school by the time they attend college. If you purchase an insurance policy with a rider for your spouse, there will be savings in the insurance cost.

Ok, so you have car insurance, health insurance, now life insurance. What other insurances should you consider? To back track, when you retire, your company may provide you with part of your retirement package health insurance up to 65. At 65, you should consider getting a medicare supplemental insurance to assist in bridging the gap in coverage of medicare. This coverage won't pay all the difference, but help defray the costs. There are several levels of coverage and you need to take the time to review which plan is right for you.

With the aging of America, and the increase in life expectancy, many seniors are finding they can't take care of themselves and go into facilities for long term care. The national average is just around 3 years. This is misleading as men tend to be what you might say a little hard headed and go later into a nursing home and have shorter stays. Females tend to stay longer in nursing homes. I had a client once that was in a home almost 15 years. He family was thankful for her oil royalties she had gotten. The national average today is a little over $ 41,000 a year. If you don't think about long term care insurance, this could deplete your retirement funds. For those of you who are married, what funds will be left for the surviving spouse if you deplete the funds while you are in a nursing home. There are estimates anywhere from 1out of 3 to about 1 out of 2 will go into a nursing home. This is a serious topic and needs to have serious discussions with your spouse and your family.

Some of you may say my spouse will take care of me, not to worry. Ok, have you thought about what quality of life you will give to your healthy spouse. They will probably be home bound, and give up many things in their retirement years for you. Sure, they do it with love, but is it the right thing to do? Also, even though they will do their best, will they provide you the proper care you need? Talk to your spouse, discuss "what if" scenarios, and be realistic about what you will do.

Some of you may say my child loves me and has offered I stay with them. That is such a wonderful gesture. But let's see, can you not be effected by the noise of their small and teenage children? How will their spouse react. Have you ever seen a tea kettle. When it get's enough steam, it explodes. Your child needs relief from being part of what is known as the sandwich generation. In simple terms, they are taking care of their children and their parents at the same time. If you have more than one child, you need to discuss this with the family. Let them know you thoughts and what you are considering planning for your potential stay in a nursing home. You also need to have all children become part of the program. If you live with one child, the other children need to hear from you that they are expected to help out from time to time to let the child you are living with get away for a weekend, a family vacation with their spouse and their children. Simply, plan different scenarios.

If you are a child and your parents are getting close to retirement, do some advanced planning. They may not be in the same city as you. Can you imagine getting a call that your parent is in the hospital and they can no longer care for themselves. Maybe you have gone home for the holidays and that emaculate home your mother kept is a house now full of clutter. Just what if, what if they need help. Plan ahead and look at the options of where they may stay. Make a folder and get information and costs ahead of time. Not during a time you are in denial that your super dad or super mom can no longer take care of themselves. Learn about programs for meals for wheels where they deliver hot meals to their home. Learn if there are visiting nurse associations that can check up weekly on your parents if they are still at home and they are aging. In my tidbit section, I have listed websites to explore, learn, and get information from.

One last insurance to look at is disability. You may have a policy through your job, but what if you get laid off, it will stop that month. You might consider having an individual policy. Most disability policies I have seen only provide about 60% of your annual income. If you don't plan for a potential disability, where will your family get funds to pay your current bills?

CHAPTER Twenty-Four
It's up to you now

In this book I have tried to give you your **"why"** in life. I will give you a hint, when I ask clients, why do they work, I usually get to pay their bills. In reality, we all work to fund the lifestyle that we want to live. I have given you exercises to make you think a little out of the box. To make you think beyond today, and for the rest of your life. Exercises to make you put down what lifestyle you want to live. I have given you tools to help you work toward the lifestyle you want to achieve. You might have noticed that I used a lot of quotes from a variety of well known people. All of us have hobbies and different interest in life. I have tried to bring you closer to the subject that most of us avoid, our financial future, by tying in famous people that are respected. What I call the "how," the investment vehicles and strategies are much easier for all of us to find and meet our objectives. Like someone reducing their weight, we all know that we need to eat healthy, and be concerned about cholesterol, heart disease, etc. But until we have our "WHY," the how can't fall in place. Using weight reduction as an example, there are several programs out there that can help each of us obtain our objective. But until we have the desire and motivation, being told how to reduce our weight is meaningless. I encourage you to reread this book. In fact, I have a favorite book I recommend, "Who Moved My Cheese" by Dr. Spencer Johnson. Maybe before your second read of my book, read that book. It is a short book, but it will help put you in a great mindset. In my future writings, I will go over the how of investing.

I would love to hear from you on how my book helped you. Feel free to send me an email at edgardner@msn.com. If you want a website to help you with your financial future, keep my website as a favorite resource, www.planningaheadwithed.com Until we meet again, or you read another book of mine, MANY HAPPY RETURNS!

Tidbits

I have had an opportunity in Houston for years to have a radio show which currently is on CNN 650 AM during Monday morning's drive time from 7:00 to 8:00 AM. On my show from time to time I give little tidbits whether it be references or ways to save money. I thought I would share a few in my last chapter. The ideas and concepts alone in this chapter should have given you more value than what the book cost you. But items in the book can and will give you opportunites to save substantially more than the cost of this book. Are you ready? Here they are:

Free 411 calls - I am sure you have been in your car, left you appointment calendar and need a number of somewhere you are going or need to contact someone. One of the most annoying thing is to have to call information and then be charged to get a phone number. Would you like to get a free 411 call? To get one, you dial 1-800-free-411, that's 1-800-373-3411. The call is always sponsored by an advertiser, so if you don't mind a few seconds of commercials, you will **save** a lot of money in the future on 411 calls.

Find lost money - Over the years you and your family may have moved when you were young, when you went to college, and when you moved for job opportunities. In your travels you may have not always notified institutions with a change of your address. After a period of time, usually two years, if an institution can't contact you, they send funds to the state treasury. You may have had a bank account, insurance policy where the insurance company demutualized, old 401k, etc and there are funds there that were never distributed to you. There is a website www.unclaimed.org. This is a national website that you will see a map of the U.S. When you see the map, you can then click your mouse on the state that you live in. You will be redirected to that states website. You can go on the website and then put your name and the city that you lived in. If there were funds in your name, they will usually list the address along with your name of any unclaimed funds that went to that states treasury. If you see your name with an address you use to reside at, you have just found unclaimed funds. Each website will tell you how to go through the process of having the funds sent to you. Most states will charge a small % for processing. I had one of my radio listeners recently call me and tell me they got a check for almost $ 1,400. It was just before Christmas and now they were able to pay cash for all their holiday gifts for family and friends. By the way, while you are checking your name, why not check your parents, brothers, sisters, and other family members. Good luck in your search.

Airline Tickets – Ever travel and find out the person next to you paid a loss less for their ticket than you. Go to www.yapta.com. You can check pricing on tickets. If you find a ticket less than what you paid for it, you can have it reissued less airline fee and possibly get a refund.

Caregiving - When a loved one becomes ill and you don't know where to go for help, below are a few websites that may be of interest

Children of Aging Parents www.caps-4caregivers.org 800 227 7294

Family Caregivers Alliance www.caregiver.org 800 445 8106

National Alliance for Caregiving www.caregiving.org 301 718 8444

National Family Caregivers Association 800 896 3650 www.nfcacares.org

Centers for Medicare & Medicaid Services *www.cms.hhs.gov* 877-267-2323 (toll-free) 866-226-1819 (TTY)

AARP *www.aarp.org* 888-687-2277

National Association of Area Agencies on Aging *www.n4a.org* 202-842-0888

National Association of State Units on Aging *www.nasua.org* 202-898-2578

National Elder Law Foundation *www.nelf.org* 520-881-1076

College assistance – If you have a child, you probably have thought about the future costs of college. It is never to early to start learning about scholarships, grants, and more. Check out these websites

    Fin Aid – www.finaid.com - guide to financial aid

    www.Fastweb.com – matching students to scholarships

    www.Collegefortexans.com

Credit bureau –
    Equiifax 800 685 1111 www.equifax.com
    Experian 800 397 3742 www.experian.com
    TransUnion 800 888 4213 www.tuc.com

Credit report - Free annual copy – www.annualcreditreport.com or 877-322-8228

Coupons – different sites to get discounts
    www.consumerworld.com
    www.coolsavings.com
    www.couponmountain.com
    www.couponpages.com
    www.freebiecat.com/couponcat.html
    www.homebasics.com
    www.hotcoupons.com
    www.refundsweepers.com
    www.smartsource.com
    www.valuepage.com
    www.couponcollect.com
    www.couponmountain.com
    www.currentcodes.com
    www.dealcatcher.com

Debt – Statue of Limitation by state - www.fair-debt-collection.com/SOL-by-State.html

Dividend paying stocks - www.better-investing.org or www.moneypaper.com

Gas prices - want to check the best gas prices in your area, go to these websites and put in your zip code www.gaspricewatch.com or www.gasbuddy.com

Golf courses – search golf courses worldwide – www.golfcourses.com

Grandparents that are taking care of your grandchildren – then get information and assistance by contacting - HTTP://GRC4USA.ORG

Identify Theft – Should you experience that you are a victim of identity theft, take the following steps as soon as possible
1. Contact the fraud department of each of the three major credit reporting bureaus. Ask that a "fraud" alert be placed in your filed and add that they add a victim statement that creditors contact you before opening a new account in your name.
   Equifax 800 525 6285
   Experian 888 397 3742
   Transunion 80 680 7289
2. Contact the security department of creditors or financial institutions of any fraudulently accessed or open account. Close the account and change passwords on any new account. Tell the creditor or institution that this is a case of id theft.
3. File a report with your local a police or where the identity theft took place. Get copy of the police report in

case the bank credit card company or other creditor needs proof of the crime later on.
4. Cancel all current checking and savings accounts and open new ones. Contact major check verification companys to alert them of theft of your checks.
    Global payments 800 766 2748
    ChexSystems 800 428 9623
    Cross check 800-552-1900
    Scan 800 262 7771
    Telecheck 800-710-9898
5. Make a report to the Federal Trade Commission Identity theft hotline (877 438 4338) or logging on to www.consumer.gov/idtheft

IPO Watch- www.ipohome.com

IRS refunds – www.irs.gov – "where's my refund". Before you call in, make sure you have your social security number, the filing status you used, and the amount of the refund. If you would rather call the IRS, call 800 829 4477.

Job Hunting - 50 and older – check out www.workforce50.com.

Job Loss - how to survive financially after job loss- national Financial Planning Association support center 800 647 6340 or www.fpanet.org free

Maps - www.mapquest.com or www.google.com/maps

Medicare hotline - 800-633-4227, www.medicare.gov

Medicare participating doctors- See who participates-800 633 4227 or by internet. www.medicare.gov Click on "Participating Physician Directory" on left side of the screen.

Nursing Home – Medicare has a website that might be helpful in finding a nursing home.
www.medicare.gov/nhcompare/home.asp

Organ Donation – www.organdonor.gov

Pension Search - www.obtc.gov- pension search program, 1200 K Street NW, Washington, DC 20005. If you have a loved one who has died, ill, or you have moved around a lot, it is wise to check to see if the person you are checking for may have had a retirement account that they had forgotten about.

Pet Trust - Learn about a trust for your pet and free info from Humane Society of the US
www.hsus.org

Postal auctions - www.usps.com, click search and then auctions. You can also contact the Atlanta Mail Recovery Center, 5345 Fulton Industrial Blvd, SW, Atlanta, Georgia

Savings Bonds - they do mature, check you value http://www.treasurydirect.gov/BC/SBCPrice or www.publicdebt.treas.gov

Socially Responsible Investing - Get information to assist you – www.socialfunds.com, www.csrwire.com,

Social Security – to get literature so you can understand benefits, ask for item 518k by calling 888 878 3256 or go to their website www.pueblo.gsa.gov. You can also contact Social Security at 800-772-1213 (hearing impaired call 800-325-0778) or by their website www.ssa.gov. Some popular publications are 05-10084 (Survivors Benefits) and publication 05-

10024(Social Security, understanding the benefits).

Student Loan Sources - www.salliemae.com and www.collegiatefunding.com

Tax Return Copy – you can always order a copy from the IRS and pay a fee. Or, you can ask for a transcript by getting Form 4506T. Get a copy at www.irs.gov or call 800-829-1040. Takes about 2 weeks.

Teaching Children about Money –
www.mymoneymanagement.net
http://curriculum.financialeducaiton.citigroup.com

Travel Overseas Refund -
Value Added Tax – up to 20% in Europe – so refunds can be significant
Refund varies by country, is complex
Global Refund – call 800 566 9828
Or visit www.globalrefund.com before you travel

Travel Warnings – travel.state.gov 888 407 4747

Free medication – If someone is low income, they could possibly be eligible for free or low cost medicines. Contact needy meds www.needymeds.com. You can also go to pharmaceutical research and manufacturers of America 800 762 4636 or www.phrma.org. If paperwork overwhelming, then contact medicine program 573 996 7300 or www.themedicineprogram.com for $ 5.00 per prescription drug requested.

Generic Drug equivalent – www.fda.gov/cder/ogd. Click on "Drug Information" or call 888 463 6332

Useful Web Links

American Stock Exchange - http://www.amex.com

AARP – www.aarp.org

Barron's - http://www.barrons.com

CNN Financial News - http://www.cnnfn.com

Fannie Mae – www.fanniemae.com

Federal Deposit Insurance Corporation – www.fdic.gov/consumers/consumer/moneysmart

Federal Reserve Board – www.federalresereeducation.org

Federal Trade Commission – www.ftc.gov

First Gov for Consumers – www.consumer.gov/yourmoney.htm

Freddie Mac – www.freddiemac.com

Get Checking – www.getchecking.org

Homeownership Preservation Foundation – www.995hope.org

Internal Revenue Service - http://irs.gov

Living to 100.com - http://www.livingto100.com

Medicare - http://www.medicare.gov

NASDAQ Stock Market - http://www.nasdaq.com

National Associaton of Insurance Commissioners – www.insureuonline.org

National Council on Economic Education – www.ncee.net

National Credit Union Administration – www.ncua.gov/consumerinformation

New York Stock Exchange - http://www.nyse.com

Operation Hope, Inc. – www.operatinhope.org

Sallie Mae – www.salliemae.com

Securities and Exchange Commision – www.sec.gov

Smart Money - http://www.smartmoney.com

Social Security Administration – http://www.socialsecurity.gov

The Street - http://www.thestreet.com Wall Street Journal – http://finance.yahoo.com

U.S. Department of the Treasury – www.treasurydirect.gov

U.S. Financial Literacy and Education Commission – www.mymoney.gov

Yahoo Finance - http://finance.yahoo.com

Edward M Gardner CPA CFP® PFS CSA MPA BBA
2519 South Blvd, Suite 100
Houston, Texas 77098
713-659-7526 (PLAN)
edgardner@msn.com
www.planningaheadwithed.com

Sometimes we just need to be reminded!

*A well-known speaker
started off his seminar by:*

*holding up a $20.00
bill. In the room of 200, he asked,
'Who would like this
$20 bill?'*

Hands started going up.

*He said, 'I am going to give this
$20 to one of you*

*but first, let me
do this.
He
proceeded to crumple up the $20 dollar bill.*

*He then asked, 'Who
still wants it?'*

*--Still the hands
were up in the air.*

*Well, he
replied, 'What if I do this?'*

*And he
dropped it on the ground*

*and started
to grind it into the floor with his shoe.*

He picked it up, now crumpled and dirty.

'Now, who still wants it?'

Still the hands went into the air.

*My friends, we have all learned a
very valuable lesson.*

*No matter what
I did to the money, you still wanted it*

*because it did not decrease in value.
It was still worth $20.*

Many times in our lives,

*we are dropped, crumpled, and ground
into the dirt*

*by the decisions we
make and*

*the circumstances that come
our way.*

*We feel as though we are
worthless.*

But no matter what has

happened or

*what will happen, you
will never lose your value.*

*Dirty or
clean, crumpled or finely creased,*

*you are still
priceless to those who DO LOVE you.*

*The worth of our
lives comes not in what we do or who we know,*

*but by WHO WE ARE and
WHOSE WE ARE.*

*You are
special
-
Don't EVER forget it.'*

*Count your blessings,
not your problems.*

*'And remember:
amateurs built the ark ..*

*professionals
built the Titanic.*

*If God brings you to
it - He will bring you through it.*

Author Unknown